Financial and Market Integration of Vulnerable People

'In Financial and Market Integration of Vulnerable People Linda Jones brings a breadth of thinking from a number of authors to engage on how the poorest can be served by market systems development and inclusive financial services. She lays out a challenge for practitioners to take sustainable approaches to work with the most vulnerable. It is up to the reader to act on the important analysis she and others have provided.'

Dan Norell, Senior Technical Advisor,
Economic Development, World Vision

'Everyone committed to understanding issues of vulnerability worldwide should read this book.'

Dr David Lawson, University of Manchester

Financial and Market Integration of Vulnerable People

Lessons from development programmes

Edited by Linda Jones

KEY WRITINGS IN ENTERPRISE
DEVELOPMENT AND MICROFINANCE

PRACTICAL ACTION
Publishing

Practical Action Publishing Ltd
The Schumacher Centre,
Bourton on Dunsmore, Rugby,
Warwickshire, CV23 9QZ, UK
www.practicalactionpublishing.org

A catalogue record for this book is available from the British Library.
A catalogue record for this book has been requested from the Library of Congress.

ISBN 978-1-85339-887-2 Hardback
ISBN 978-1-85339-888-9 Paperback
ISBN 978-1-78044-887-9 Library Ebook
ISBN 978-1-78044-888-6 Ebook

Citation: Jones, L. (ed.) (2015) *Financial and Market Integration of Vulnerable People: Lessons from development programmes*, Rugby, UK: Practical Action Publishing, <http://dx.doi.org/10.3362/9781780448879>

Since 1974, Practical Action Publishing has published and disseminated books and information in support of international development work throughout the world. Practical Action Publishing is a trading name of Practical Action Publishing Ltd (Company Reg. No. 1159018), the wholly owned publishing company of Practical Action. Practical Action Publishing trades only in support of its parent charity objectives and any profits are covenanted back to Practical Action (Charity Reg. No. 247257, Group VAT Registration No. 880 9924 76).

The views and opinions in this publication are those of the author and do not represent those of Practical Action Publishing Ltd or its parent charity Practical Action. Reasonable efforts have been made to publish reliable data and information, but the authors and publisher cannot assume responsibility for the validity of all materials or for the consequences of their use.

Typeset by Allzone Digital Services Limited
Printed in the UK

FSC

Contents

http://dx.doi.org/10.3362/9781780448879.000

About the editor

Linda Jones is an internationally recognized consultant in applying market systems approaches (value chains, financial systems, M4P, PSD) to inclusive economic development programmes that successfully leverage the contributions of women, smallholder farmers and other vulnerable groups. Dr Jones works globally with multiple clients and donors, and is currently directing MEDA's work in investment-led development.

CHAPTER 1

Introduction: integrating vulnerable people into financial and market systems

Linda Jones

Abstract

This introductory chapter starts by examining how we define poverty and destitution, including the Human Development Index and the Multidimensional Poverty Index. It considers which groups of people are most likely to be poor and vulnerable; they are often smallholder farmers, women, young people, people with disability, excluded minorities and the entrenched poor. It goes on to outline the chapters, debates and programmatic approaches that follow, including the use of smart subsidy, cash transfers, savings groups and the push–pull approach.

Keywords: financial inclusion; value chains; Human Development Index; Multidimensional Poverty Index; destitution; poverty

Introduction

This book presents experiences from development programmes on the integration of vulnerable people into financial and market systems (including value chains) through development programming.

Smallholder farmers, women earners, young job-seekers, people with disability and the entrenched poor often struggle to sustain themselves or contribute to the wellbeing of their households. Despite our knowledge of this situation, and our collective desire to remedy it, microfinance and enterprise development programmes have repeatedly been unable to reach the most vulnerable for a variety of reasons discussed throughout this volume. At the same time, some programmes and approaches are making advances, and the writings included here provide conceptual and practical insights into how we can contribute more to the wellbeing of those most in need. First, however, we turn to an examination of who the most vulnerable are and where they can be found (MEDA, 2014).

How do we define poverty?

In order to know who is vulnerable, it is helpful to understand poverty in general – how do we define poverty, where are the poor clustered, and how can we characterize the lives of the most vulnerable? The commonly used

http://dx.doi.org/10.3362/9781780448879.001

UNDP Human Development Index (HDI) ranks countries across dimensions: health, education, and income. However, HDI is a 'summary measure of average achievement across measures' and 'does not reflect on inequalities, poverty, human security, empowerment, etc.' (UNDP, 2014a). The World Bank's US$1.25 (PPP)[1] per capita per day measure of absolute poverty is also widely used (including in the HDI) and is helpful for understanding which households are the poorest in terms of income.[2] But both the HDI and $1.25 PPP are lacking when we consider the multi-dimensional characteristics of individual household poverty. For example, although Ethiopia and Uzbekistan both reported about 50 per cent of the population living under $1.25 per day in 2010 'by multidimensional measures that capture living standards, almost 90 per cent of Ethiopians live in poverty, while only a small percentage of Uzbekistanis do' (Morrell, 2011).

Therefore, in order to reflect the reality of people's lives and to determine which households are poor, Oxford University and UNDP introduced the Multidimensional Poverty Index (MPI) in 2010 that assesses non-income factors across three key areas of deprivation applied at the individual level: health, education and living standards (OPHI, 2014a). Although not all countries report on the necessary metrics, about half of the countries covered (91 of 187) in the 2014 UNDP *Human Development Report* are assessed according to the MPI (OPHI, 2014b).

Consolidated findings in 2014 (OPHI, 2014a) reveal that 1.6 billion people are considered to be 'MPI-poor', with 85 per cent living in rural areas (Alkire et al., 2014a). Of the world's poorest countries, the bottom 10 on both the MPI and HDI are in sub-Saharan Africa (UNDP, 2014b). In fact, out of a total of 30 countries with over half of their population MPI-poor (in those countries for whom data are available), only 6 are outside sub-Saharan Africa: Pakistan, India, Lao PDR, Philippines, Timor-Leste and Yemen. According to HDI, four of the six – India, Lao, Timor-Leste, Philippines – are rated at a middle level of human development, revealing significant disparities in the vulnerabilities of people within these countries.

The existence of widespread destitution – even among middle-income countries – is supported by the MPI which describes a standard of living for the destitute that is shockingly low and includes half of the MPI poor. As of the writing of this introduction, MPI reports found that over 638 million people are destitute across only 49 countries analysed thus far with India accounting for about half of the destitute (28.5 per cent of the Indian population). The following are selected statistics on the world's destitute households (Alkire et al. 2014b):

- 46% of the destitute do not have anyone in their home with more than one year of schooling;
- 36% of the destitute have a primary-aged school child out of school;
- 41% of the destitute live in a household in which at least one woman/man has lost two or more children;
- 67% of the destitute have someone at home with severe malnutrition;

- 71% of the destitute don't have electricity to turn on their lights;
- 90% of the destitute practise open defecation to relieve themselves;
- 40% of the destitute don't have clean water, or must walk 45 minutes to get it;
- All of the destitute are deprived in at least one-third of the weighted indicators.

Deep and widespread poverty also exists in urban centres. When we raise the poverty bar to $2 PPP per day or even $10 per day and consider the cost of living in a city, then a very different poverty picture emerges. For example, the ADB reports that in Asia about one third of city dwellers live in slums or sub-standard housing and urban environments are often congested, unhealthy and lacking in social supports (ADB, 2013).

Who are the poor and vulnerable?

Within the poorest segments of society, smallholder farmers, women, youth, people with disability, discriminated ethnicities and other excluded groups are over-represented.

- The MPI reports that the majority of the rural poor earn their living from agriculture, which is supported by the 2013 World Bank study on poverty: 'not surprisingly, a large share of the poor (63 per cent) are working in agriculture – mostly smallholder farming (Olinto et al., 2013).'
- Women's poverty is often related to access: the FAO reports that women carry out almost half of agricultural work but have greatly reduced access to inputs, services, markets, and finance (FAO, 2014), resulting in significant lost income for their households (whether joint or female headed).
- Ethnic groups may be excluded from economic benefit: OPHI has found through its MPI index that even among the poor whose lot has been improving, certain ethnicities – such as the Peuhl in Benin and the Guan in Ghana – may be left out as poverty is reduced (Alkire and Vaz, 2014).
- People with disabilities often face external barriers to participation: the ILO promotes economic inclusion of people with disabilities demonstrating that when social and physical barriers are addressed, people with disabilities contribute to society as a whole (ILO, 2014).
- Youth are massively unemployed and underemployed. In 2013, the ILO reported on a generation of youth at risk due to high youth populations and extreme unemployment with up to two-thirds of youth underutilized in some economies (ILO, 2013).

Moreover, the most vulnerable people often bear the brunt of advancement – unfortunately not usually their own development – eking out a livelihood in a degraded environment and most affected by climate change. Further, they are frequently found in countries that are beset by corruption, conflict, natural disasters and other disabling phenomena.

The world's vulnerable people are therefore a vast segment of society, concentrated in sub-Saharan Africa, and South and South-east Asia (but not only in these regions). They live in both middle- and low-income countries; most are rural, but urban poverty is also severe; they are smallholder farmers, women, youth, people with disability, excluded minorities and the entrenched poor; and half of the poor are destitute suffering extreme deprivation – with few skills, virtually no assets, low education and very little to enable them to become participants in the mainstream economy.

This book reports on the experience of microfinance and enterprise development programmes in integrating vulnerable populations into mainstream economies, and for the most part illustrates that a 'leg-up' of some kind is normally required. That is, with too few resources and assets of any kind, meagre market information and knowledge, limited access to opportunities, frequently high transaction costs due to weak infrastructure and long distances, and no clear path for engaging with markets, vulnerable people require supports that go beyond the typical microfinance and enterprise development initiatives. This viewpoint is not new, but there is significant growing awareness, programming and formalization of methodologies that offer additional supports to enable more vulnerable people engage in financial and market systems.

The chapters

The chapters collected here explore many of the vulnerabilities described above, cut across Africa, Asia and Latin America, and cover topics as diverse as: non-financial support for very poor would-be microfinance clients, credit barriers for people living with disabilities, capacity building and localized support for women microentrepreneurs, development of pro-poor value chains for smallholder farmers and self-determination of indigenous peoples in terms of economic resources. We now turn to a brief discussion of each chapter and its relevance to the inclusion of vulnerable populations in financial and market systems.

The first two chapters offer an examination of different types of graduation models for the financial inclusion of the poorest. Zimmerman and Holmes (2015), positing cash transfers as the first step to financial inclusion, turn the whole notion of the bad subsidy on its head. Subsidies had been considered poor practice in market systems programmes in the early 2000s, followed by a loosening of practitioner opinion that led to 'smart' subsidies being acceptable if they were time-bound, non-distortionary and transparent (see for example: Jeans, Fowler and Osorio, 2011). During the same time, microfinance institutions had become increasingly risk averse, focusing on operational sustainability and lending mainly to those hovering around the poverty line rather than below it (Hashemi and Montesquiou, 2011).

Zimmerman and Holmes discuss the value of cash transfers in poverty reduction for the very poor – typically provided by national governments – when tied to savings and delivered by efficient electronic payments. Although not usually linked to financial services, Zimmerman and Holmes explain the benefits for recipients when the cash transfers are linked to savings: improved management of assets, consumption smoothing and increased resiliency to shocks. They review savings-linked social protection models and suggest that this approach has the power to 'provide an even more effective and efficient means of protecting and empowering the most vulnerable populations (Ibid, p.13).' The chapter provides strong statistical evidence for the efficacy of cash transfer when linked with savings, and with the use of new technologies. Zimmerman and others have also worked on the electronic delivery aspects of cash transfers, and while benefits are clear, there are challenges that impede successful outcomes. For example, Zimmerman et al. (2014) found that in Brazil, Mexico, Colombia and South Africa that country readiness and the technical capacity to shift to electronic payments may not be up to the required level; design and security issues remain a concern; and recipients may need further support and trust building to benefit from electronic payments (Zimmerman, 2014).

Taking a different tack, Grameen (Druschel et al., 2015) proposes a graduation model for the poorest that combines financial product development, livelihoods support and value chain approaches. In this model, transfer of assets or cash may not be necessary, the emphasis being upon sequencing of capacity development – e.g. confidence and entrepreneurship – alongside linkages to economic opportunities. Grameen draws key conclusions from research with RUMA in Indonesia, Fonkoze in Haiti, BASIX and Unitus in India, and M-Pesa in Kenya among others. These lessons illustrate that there is a business case for working with the very poor, that the poorest households require more hands-on support, that market-systems approaches must be rigorous in their inclusion of the poor at different steps in the value chain, and that savings combined with the use of technology are critical for the very poor.

Although only touched on in these two chapters, savings groups – in particular, village savings and loan associations (VSLAs) promoted by CARE and Oxfam among others – have received widespread attention as an impactful avenue for financial inclusion of the poorest. Jeffrey Ashe, a pioneer in the savings movement, reports that ten million people in the world now have access to savings, and that this revolutionizes not only financial inclusion but development of the poorest – smoothing consumption, investing in other livelihood activities, empowering women, and more (Ashe and Neilan, 2014; Jones, 2015). Similar lessons are reported in various articles from *Enterprise Development and Microfinance* journal including (Hendricks and Chidiac, 2011; Proaño et al., 2011, Ledgerwood and Wilson, 2013).

The next two chapters offer insights into the challenges for financial inclusion of a highly vulnerable target group – people with disabilities. Often stigmatized, isolated, without needed supports, and viewed as non-contributors, people with disabilities are rarely included in economic development programmes. In order to promote access to financial services for people with disabilities, Leymat (2015) examines the process for designing and delivering the most appropriate products. The author concludes that complementary partnership development between microfinance actors and organizations serving people with disabilities is the best alternative for project success. The chapter also stresses that people with disabilities want a fair shot at access to financial services – that handouts are not a permanent answer and that they are ready to take on this challenge. The Beisland and Mersland chapter (2015) supports Leymat's findings, providing an in-depth example from Uganda which asserts that the greatest obstacle in accessing finance for people with disabilities is product design. Although not the only barrier, if products were more 'disability friendly', there would be greater uptake by people with disabilities. Like Leymat's, this chapter also underlines the value of working with organizations for people with disabilities.

In the following set of three chapters, we look at the case of the rural poor, especially smallholder farmers – their vulnerabilities, risks and opportunities. In the first of this group, Stoian et al. (2015) questions the growing trend for value chain development projects, cautioning that such initiatives are commonly based on the assumptions that poor households have sufficient resources to participate effectively in value chain development, do not face substantial trade-offs when using up resources for value chain activities, and are able to assume higher risks when reinvesting capital and labour. In reality, they remind us, many poor households reduce risk by pursuing diversified livelihood strategies that combine subsistence and market-oriented agriculture with off-farm labour and other non-agricultural income-generating activities. Therefore, the authors suggest that selecting a single value chain for investment of money and time may not produce the desired poverty alleviation goals, and that programmes should adopt an asset-based approach to understand households and to build capacities for value chain integration as appropriate.

Proponents of the value chain approach were aware of the challenges of working with the very poor, and programmes were designed to experiment with new models to gainfully include poorer farmers into market systems. MEDA had conducted a programme in Zambia that supported smallholders in the acquisition of productive technologies, that recognized the risks faced by these farmers (Snelgrove and Manje, 2015). The chapter reports that poor farmers are disinclined to purchase new technologies, while manufacturers, wholesalers and retailers are unwilling to invest in inventory to sell to such farmers. To remedy this situation, MEDA went against best practice at the time and introduced subsidies (in the form of discount vouchers) to accelerate demand and supply for critical production technologies. The thesis of the initiative was that properly administered incentives would attract commercial suppliers to actively address the needs of rural, underserved smallholder farmers. To further reduce risk for farmers and bolster demand, the programme offered training sessions on the use of new technologies (in this case micro-irrigation), did not limit the use of the incentive to a single specific product, and enabled farmers to make informed decisions about the use of subsidies and the purchase of farming equipment.

More recently, USAID's LEO project implemented by ACDI/VOCA (2014), has tested and promoted a combined strategy that both builds capacities, assets and resilience to 'push' the very poor into markets and also develops market linkages and other links and services that 'pull' them into markets. The push–pull approach, as it is called, recognizes that vulnerable people have unique needs and are not always able to take advantage of opportunities that are created through market systems approaches. The intentionality of combining both push and pull strategies, and an exploration of what this means in projects is currently underway (SEEP Network, 2014). The next chapter presents a push–pull case for the integration of smallholder farmers into markets in Tanzania. The following chapter is also informed by push–pull, but describes market engagement of women in different sectors in Afghanistan, Pakistan and Ghana.

Walkerman (2015) explores how push–pull techniques are implemented by the Aga Khan Foundation (AKF) in Tanzania. In many environments in which AKF works, there is not a direct, natural link between small-scale producers and lead firms that can result in a stable market linkage. On the producers' side, there are constraints around volume, quality, time, and even a lack of interest in developing long-term direct relationships with a company. As for the lead firms, they are rarely able to deal directly with large numbers of fragmented smallholder farmers. While every context demands unique tactics and models, AKF's experience suggests that local entrepreneurs – business-minded people active in their own community – can play a central role in connecting producers and lead firms, pushing farmers into markets with various supports and then creating the market pull through linkages to lead firms.

The final two chapters deal with two other vulnerable populations: women and indigenous people. The first of these two illustrates how push–pull approaches have also been effective in working with women who face significant constraints in engaging with markets. Faveri et al. (2015) presents case studies on how MEDA Ghana, ECDI Pakistan and Zardozi Afghanistan have dealt with pervasive socio-cultural, economic and enabling environment barriers that inhibit women's participation in the productive sphere, and particularly their entry into market systems. They articulate the importance of 'push' strategies – skills development, confidence building, subsidies, awareness raising – to help women producers overcome persistent gender-based discrimination that limits access to opportunities and resources, while disempowering women in their decision-making and life choices. At the same time, the authors show how the implementation of deliberate 'pull' strategies – market linkages, access to finance, input supplies – can lead to greater scale, reach and sustainability through market integration.

In the last chapter of the book, Tanaka (2015) draws on the experience of indigenous people and community forest industries in Mexico and Guatemala. The author makes the case that that producer agency rather than donors' agendas should drive initiatives, and that the vision of an enterprise should be guided by buyers' values. This is a shift from a 'farmer first' to 'customer first' culture that the author argues is of paramount importance for successful programming. The two case studies elaborated in the chapter provide evidence to support the author's case, with one case more driven and the other more buyer-oriented but 'owned' by the producers.

The volume closes with a debate between Linda Jones and Ben Fowler, tackling the questions: if and how the poorest can be reached, and what can be done by development organizations? They discuss recent approaches to targeting vulnerable populations and their level of success.

In sum, the chapters in this volume add evidence to the argument that, where vulnerable populations are concerned, direct support may be ultimately more effective than 'trickle down'. Reducing discrimination and exploitation, redistributing even a small percentage of wealth in the world, and doing so in a considered, responsible manner will go a long way to improving our aid effectiveness.

About the author

Linda Jones is an internationally recognized consultant in applying market systems approaches (value chains, financial systems, M4P, PSD) to inclusive economic development programmes that successfully leverage the contributions of women, smallholder farmers and other vulnerable groups. Dr Jones works globally with multiple clients and donors, and is currently directing MEDA's work in investment-led development.

Endnotes

1. PPP = purchasing power parity. A calculation used to rationalize inter-country income comparisons.
2. The $1.25 per capita per day means that a household with many dependents and only one or two adults earning will be considered much poorer than a household with one or two adult earners and fewer dependents. Income is calculated by averaging across all members of the household, with some countries counting children under 14 or under 18 as a half adult equivalent.

References

ACDI/VOCA (2014) 'Global Leveraging Economic Opportunities' [webpage] <http://www.acdivoca.org/site/ID/Global-LEO-Leveraging-Economic-Opportunities> [Accessed 27 January 2015].

ADB (2013) 'Urban Poverty in Asia', [webpage] Asian Development Bank <http://www.adb.org/projects/documents/urban-poverty-asia> [Accessed 30 January 2015].

Alkire, S., Chatterjee, M., Conconi, A., Seth, S. and Vaz. A.(2014a) *Poverty in Rural and Urban Areas* Technical Note, Oxford, OPHI <http://www.ophi.org.uk/wp-content/uploads/Poverty-in-Rural-and-Urban-Areas-Direct-Comparisons-using-the-Global-MPI-2014.pdf?0a8fd7> [Accessed 30 January 2015].

Alkire, S., Chatterjee, M., Conconi, A., Seth, S. and Vaz. A. (2014b) *Who and Where are the Poorest of the Poor?* Technical note, Oxford, OPHI <http://www.ophi.org.uk/wp-content/uploads/Destitution-Who-and-Where-are-the-Poorest-of-the-Poor.pdf?0a8fd7> [Accessed 3 February 2015].

Alkire, S. and Vaz. A. (2014) Reducing Multidimensional Poverty and Destitution. Technical note, Oxford, OPHI <http://www.ophi.org.uk/wp-content/uploads/ReducingMultidimensionalPovertyandDestitution-Paceand Patterns.pdf?0a8fd7> [Accessed 3 February 2015]

Ashe, J. and Neilan, K. (2014) *In Their Own Hands: How savings groups are revolutionizing development,* San Francisco: Berrett-Koehler.

Beisland, L. and Mersland, R. (2015) 'Barriers to microcredit for disabled persons: Evidence from economically active persons in Uganda' in Jones, L. (ed.) *Financial and Market Integration of Vulnerable People: Lessons from development programmes,* Rugby: Practical Action <http://dx.doi.org/10.3362/9781780448879.005>.

Griffin, K. and Tolat, M. (2015) 'Myths, misconceptions, and the emerging truth in serving very poor households: Grameen Foundation's experience to date' in Jones, L. (ed.) *Financial and Market Integration of Vulnerable People: Lessons from development programmes, Rugby: Practical Action* <http://dx.doi.org/10.3362/9781780448879.003>.

FAO (2014) *The State of Food and Agriculture,* Rome: Food and Agriculture Organization,. <http://www.fao.org/3/a-i4040e.pdf> [Accessed February 1, 2015].

Faveri, C., Shaikh, P. and Wilson, K. (2015) 'Making markets work for women: How push and pull strategies can support women's economic empowerment' in Jones, L. (ed.) *Financial and Market Integration of Vulnerable People: Lessons from development programmes,* Rugby: Practical Action <http://dx.doi.org/10.3362/9781780448879.009>.

Fowler, B. and Jones, L. (2015) 'Can the poorest be helped by any of our current models of economic development from graduation approaches to market development?' in Jones, L. (ed.) *Financial and Market Integration of Vulnerable People: Lessons from development programmes,* Rugby: Practical Action <http://dx.doi.org/10.3362/9781780448879.011>.

Hashemi, S. and de Montesquiou, A. (2011) 'Reaching the poorest: Lessons from the graduation model', *CGAP Focus Note* No. 69. <http://www.cgap.org/sites/default/files/CGAP-Focus-Note-Reaching-the-Poorest-Lessons-from-the-Graduation-Model-Mar-2011.pdf> [Accessed 29 January 2015].

Hendricks, Lauren and Chidiac, Sybil (2011) 'Village savings and loans: A pathway to financial inclusion for Africa's poorest households' *Enterprise Development and Microfinance* 22(2) pp.134-46, <http://dx.doi.org/10.3362/1755-1986.2011.016>

ILO (2013) *Global Employment Trends for Youth 2013: A generation at risk,* Geneva: International Labour Office, <http://www.ilo.org/wcmsp5/groups/public/@dgreports/@dcomm/documents/publication/wcms_212423.pdf> [Accessed 4 February 2015].

ILO (2014) 'Breaking the vicious circle of disability and extreme poverty'. Brief for International Day for the Eradication of Poverty 2014, ILO-Irish Aid Partnership Programme on Disability <http://www.ilo.org/wcmsp5/groups/public/---ed_emp/---ifp_skills/documents/event/wcms_313833.pdf> [Accessed 28 January, 2015].

Jeans, A., Fowler, B. and Osorio, L. (2011) 'Synthesis of the Online Discussion: Smart subsidies in market facilitation', a SEEP Network Online Discussion hostedbytheMarketFacilitationInitiative(MaFI).<http://www.slideshare.net /marketfacil/smart-subsidies-in-akis-final-mar2011-7192114> [Accessed 29 January 2015].

Jones, L. (2015) Book review of Ashe and Neilan (2014) in *Enterprise Development and Microfinance* 26 (1): 75-6.

Ledgerwood, Joanna and Wilson, Kim (2013) 'Community-based financial services: a spectrum of providers', *Enterprise Development and Microfinance* 24(2) <http://dx.doi.org/10.3362/1755-1986. 2013.010>

Leymat, A. (2015) 'Inclusive Microfinance: Reaching disabled people through partnership development' in Jones, L. (ed.) *Financial and Market Integration of Vulnerable People: Lessons from development programmes,* Rugby: Practical Action <http://dx.doi.org/10.3362/9781780448879.004>.

MEDA (2014) 'Trends in international economic development: challenges and opportunities', internal report prepared by L. Jones, and referenced with permission of MEDA, Mennonite Economic Development Associates.

Morrell, D. (2011) 'Qualitative measures: Who is poor?' in *Harvard Magazine* http://harvardmagazine.com/2011/01/who-is-poor [Accessed 2 February 2015].

OPHI (2014a) 'The Oxford Poverty and Human Development Initiative' [website], Oxford: Oxford Department of International Development, http://www.ophi.org.uk/multidimensional-poverty-index/mpi-2014/ [Accessed 3 February 2015].

OPHI (2014b) 'Country briefings', [website], Oxford: Oxford Department of International Development, http://www.ophi.org.uk/multidimensional-poverty-index/mpi-2014/mpi-country-briefings/ [Accessed 3 February 2015].

Olinto, P., Beegle, K., Sobrado, C., and Uematsu, H. (2013) *The State of the Poor: Where Are The Poor, Where Is Extreme Poverty Harder to End, and What Is the Current Profile of the World's Poor?* The World Bank, Poverty Reduction and Economic Management Network, Washington <http://siteresources.worldbank.org/EXTPREMNET/Resources/EP125.pdf> [Accessed 4 February 2015].

Proaño, Laura Fleischer, Gash, Megan and Kuklewicz, Amelia (2011) 'Durability of savings group programmes: A decade of experience in Ecuador' *Enterprise Development and Microfinance* 22(2) pp.145-60, <http://dx.doi.org/10.3362/ 1755-1986.2011.017>

SEEP Network (2014) *USAID Calls for Practitioner Learning from Push/Pull and Inclusive Market Development* <http://www.seepnetwork.org/blog/leo-call-project-examples-inclusive-market-development-2> [Accessed 28 January 2015].

Snelgrove, A. and Manje, L. (2015) 'Catalysts of agricultural supply markets: The case for smart subsidies in Zambia' in Jones, L. (ed.) *Financial and Market Integration of Vulnerable People: Lessons from development programmes,* Rugby: Practical Action <http://dx.doi.org/10.3362/9781780448879.007>.

Stoian, D., Donovan, J., Fisk, J., and Muldoon, M. (2015) "Value chain development for rural poverty reduction: A reality check and a warning', in Jones, L. (ed.) *Financial and Market Integration of Vulnerable People: Lessons from development programmes,* Rugby: Practical Action <http://dx.doi. org/10.3362/9781780448879.006>.

Tanaka, H. (2015) 'Whose vision counts? The formulation of vision in community forest enterprises' in Jones, L. (ed.) *Financial and Market Integration of Vulnerable People: Lessons from development programmes*, Rugby: Practical Action <http://dx.doi.org/10.3362/9781780448879.010>.

UNDP (2014a) Human Development Index (HDI) [webpage] <http://hdr.undp.org/en/content/human-development-index-hdi> [Accessed 1 February, 2014].

UNDP (2014b) UNDP Human Development Report 2014. United Nations Development Programme. <http://hdr.undp.org/en/2014-report> [Accessed 1 February 2015].

Walkerman, S. (2015) 'Bringing together push and pull through local entrepreneurs: a case study from Tanzania' in Jones, L. (ed.) *Financial and Market Integration of Vulnerable People: Lessons from development programmes*, Rugby: Practical Action <http://dx.doi.org/10.3362/9781780448879.008>.

Zimmerman, J. and Homes, J. (2015) 'The G2P Opportunity: Five reasons why now is the time to leverage social protection to enable financial inclusion and savings amongst the poor' in Jones, L. (ed.) *Financial and Market Integration of Vulnerable People: Lessons from development programmes*, Rugby: Practical Action.

Zimmerman, J., Bohling, K. and Parker, S. (2014) 'Electronic G2P Payments: Evidence from Four Lower-Income Countries' *CGAP Focus Note* No. 93, Washington D.C, CGAP <http://www.cgap.org/sites/default/files/Focus-Note-Electronic-G2P-Payments-April-2014.pdf> [Accessed at 30 January 2014].

CHAPTER 2

The G2P opportunity: five reasons why now is the time to leverage social protection to enable financial inclusion and savings among the poorest

Jamie M. Zimmerman and Jamie Holmes

Abstract

Around the world, increasingly widespread cash-based social protection schemes – programmes delivering cash payments to over 750 million people among the world's most vulnerable populations – are creating opportunities, particularly through new delivery mechanisms. Policymakers and experts working in financial inclusion, social policy, human development, and behavioural economics have expressed wide interest in leveraging this shift in delivery approaches by incorporating mechanisms that either enable or encourage savings behaviour. Growing, albeit relatively limited, global evidence suggests that linking social protection payments (commonly referred to as government-to-person (G2P) payments) to savings opportunities has trifold benefits. Financial intermediaries benefit from regular infusions of cash and new clients; the recipients gain access to the tools to manage their assets and save for investments, smooth consumption, and create a savings buffer to protect against adverse events; and governments achieve improved efficiency in payments through electronic delivery and multiplier effects through enhanced developmental impact. In this paper we posit that the financial inclusion field faces a unique and important opportunity for deeper exploration of the potential benefits of direct savings-linked G2P payments for developing world governments, financial intermediaries, and most vitally, the clients themselves.

Keywords: cash transfers, social protection, goverment-to-person, vulnerable population, savings, delivery mechanisms

The last decades have seen microfinance's remarkably rapid expansion across the global South. During this period, financial services for the poor have made real inroads. However, recently, and perhaps inevitably, global development circles have also explored the failures of microfinance organizations to reach the poorest and most vulnerable.

One of the challenges is the so-called 'mission drift', in which microfinance institutions (MFIs) target borrowers that are most likely to repay, while the

http://dx.doi.org/10.3362/9781780448879.002

poorest and most vulnerable are excluded. As Syed M. Hashemi and Aude de Montesquiou wrote in March, most 'of the world's estimated 150 million microcredit clients are thought to live just below and, more often, just above the poverty line' (Hashemi and Montesquiou, 2011). While there have undoubtedly been positive impacts on poverty alleviation and gender empowerment, it is clear that microcredit alone is not always the most appropriate tool for reaching the most marginalized populations.

Although informal self-help groups have made some progress in filling the finance void, they are not adequate to address the longer-term social, economic, and political exclusion that these populations tend to suffer. However, there is a high-leverage opportunity area that the field until very recently has ignored: cash transfers to the world's most vulnerable populations.

Cash transfers to the poor are increasingly popular but suboptimal

Cash transfers to the poor, most often deployed by national governments and sometimes deployed by international donors and commonly referred to as government-to-person (G2P) payments, have become increasingly successful at targeting and reaching the ultra-poor, and the impacts of these programmes on poverty have been impressive (Hanlon et al., 2010). Conditional and unconditional cash transfers have by-and-large replaced the more traditional strategies of in-kind aid. In most cases, however, the delivery methods of these transfers are suboptimal; armoured cars with mobile ATMs, lottery offices or post offices are often operationally expensive to utilize for payments (Jackelen and Zimmerman et al., 2011).

These G2P cash-transfer programmes increasingly offer the opportunity of greater efficiency and effectiveness as they move toward various means of electronic delivery, reducing leakage and programmatic costs. E-payments have proven to significantly decrease overhead costs and reduce the corruption associated with cash payments. In India, the government is poised to save roughly $23 bn a year, according to a 2010 McKinsey report, by shifting to e-payments, with most of that saving coming from reduced leakage. At the same time, the implementation of biometric identification technology across the developing world holds the potential to address some of the regulatory hurdles to banking the ultra-poor. Debit and smart cards, mobile banking, and retail banking are among the various avenues that governments are beginning to employ to reach even the poorest and most vulnerable communities.

Despite this rapid progress, however, less than a quarter of existing cash-transfer programmes are linked to a financially inclusive bank account (Pickens et al., 2009). Digitized delivery of social protection payments using models that enable and in some cases encourage savings behaviour would allow for mutual reinforcement of social protection and financial inclusion goals, while facilitating wealth creation among millions of the world's poorest.

The G2P opportunity

Both movements – of technological advancements in financial inclusion, as well as the shift to cash payments in social protection programmes and policies – suggest that one solution to the challenge of reaching the most vulnerable poor with financial services is to leverage G2P programmes for formal savings opportunities. Savings-linked social protection transfers, by providing opportunities to build wealth, can help clients to smooth consumption and accumulate assets while building their human capital, thereby moving to escape, rather than alleviate, poverty (Zimmerman and Moury, 2009).

This paper makes the case that savings-linked social protection programmes provide a unique and timely means to effectively and efficiently provide appropriate savings services to the poorest. First, the authors detail five current global trends that present the field of financial services for the poor with the opportunity to advance savings opportunities through G2P schemes. In this context, the authors examine the conceptual framework for savings-linked social protection, including various delivery models and evidence. The authors then discuss the various policy and practical challenges that still inhibit savings-linked social protection, including various questions that remain for further examination, and next steps.

The five trends shaping the G2P opportunity

Government-to-person (G2P) social protection payments are under-going a period of transformation and transition, as new technologies are changing the traditional delivery channels, and while the evidence of the success of social protection transfers themselves are garnering the attention of the development community and broader public. Even in the face of the global economic meltdown, five trends in particular are poised to shape the future of social protection programmes, as well as the field's ability to capitalize on them to achieve financial inclusion goals: promotion, investigation, innovation, exploration, and momentum.

Promotion

The precise role of social protection in promoting better livelihoods and sustained poverty reduction is in transition; social protection is seen not merely as a means to mitigate poverty, but also as a way to help build a basis for long-term poverty alleviation. Two pillars of this new approach are the rise of conditional cash-transfer programmes, which attach conditionalities on payments that target the next generation – for example, in educational attendance requirements or health clinic visits and immunizations – and a new emphasis on the role of asset building.

While income level was traditionally used as the standard measure of poverty, interventions emphasized supplemental income to meet subsistence demands in the short term. The long-term goal of social assistance, however, is to help families move out of poverty on a permanent basis. The 'promotion' aspects of social protection, gaining increasing currency among aid professionals, emphasize this goal: income growth, and the capacity to invest in oneself, one's family, and one's future. Over the last decade, this new emphasis has led to a shift in understanding toward a broader social protection agenda that includes asset accumulation as an essential component.

In particular, there has been increased attention on the role of savings in promoting a sustainable graduation agenda. Not only can savings, as a key form of asset accumulation, protect families against shocks and help smooth consumption, they also lend themselves to long-term investments and income growth.

Investigation

Another important trend is the shift and push toward more standardized, rigorous evaluation and dissemination of the results, benefits, and challenges facing social protection programmes. With few other anti-poverty schemes of late having been subjected to such exhaustive evaluation, increased investigation of cash-transfer programmes offers the field a fuller understanding of the various costs and benefits of such schemes.

Some of the most compelling evidence of the benefits of social protection programmes comes from rigorous evaluations of conditional cash-transfer programmes. In Brazil and Mexico, such social protection programmes have cost these governments less than one half of a per cent of national income, and yet they have been responsible for roughly 21 per cent of the reduction of inequality over the last decade, according to one evaluation (Soares, et al., 2007).

Mexico's social protection programme saw poverty reduced by over 8 per cent over its tenure. The Oportunidades programme has also provided evidence that social protection schemes can help increase savings, and that the severity of poverty fell by nearly 35 per cent in their programmes (Soares, F.V. et al., 2007).

In Malawi, one study of 3,800 girls and young women in a social protection programme saw a 60 per cent drop in HIV infection rates compared with a control group after one year. There was also a 75 per cent drop in herpes infections. As the size of the transfer grew, the young women in the programme chose safer, younger sexual partners (World Bank, 2010).

Innovation

Perhaps the most prominent trend in social protection programmes is the harnessing of new technologies, and the use of new channels and delivery options. New technologies are allowing us to rethink the possibilities for delivering G2P payments, with strong implications for financial inclusion of the poor as well as efficiency of transfers and the business case for financial inclusion.

The recent explosion in agent and mobile banking is, in some contexts, significantly reducing the costs of delivering financial services. The high costs of in-person, small-balance transactions that make such accounts untenable in traditional bricks-and-mortar banks no longer stand as barriers to true expansion of financial inclusion to some of the most poor and vulnerable populations (Mas, 2011).

The sheer speed of technological innovation in the developing world today, with not only the mobile web and mobile banking but other applications such as basic mobile phones, is allowing individuals and even entire nations to leapfrog old barriers to development. In addition to mobile banking and other applications relevant to financial inclusion, these innovations are helping forge new relationships between governments and citizens by way of mobile government applications. Technological breakthroughs are also increasing levels of entrepreneurship.

The evidence of the success of e-payments is impressive. In Brazil's Bolsa Família programme, the cost of administering the grants as a proportion of the value of the grant was reduced by over 80 per cent – to 2.5 per cent of the value of the grant dispersed (Lindert et al., 2007). In Argentina, clients of one programme reported a huge drop in bribes paid to receive benefits, amounting to a total of $10.7 m saved (Consultative Group to Assist the Poor, 2008). In South Africa, delivery costs fell by over 60 per cent after private banks were made government partners (Ibid.).

Exploration

A fourth salient trend in social protection programmes has been the exploration of new ideas to make programmes more effective and efficient. One such exploration has involved the incorporation of perspectives from psychology and behavioural economics. Complementary to an assets perspective, new research has suggested that one way to further leverage social protection payments is to bear in mind, in the design of programmes, that difficult financial decisions may be mentally and emotionally draining. As over a decade of research from social psychology shows, trade-off decisions, such as whether to pay rent or buy medicine, can cause mental fatigue, with financial trade-off decisions looming constantly over the most poor and vulnerable populations.

Such insights suggest that social protection programmes can make savings interventions more effective by providing complementary services; that simply by decreasing stress in one area, behaviours such as establishing savings habits can be made easier. In one study of Mexico's programme Oportunidades, researchers found that the stress levels of families three years in the programme were significantly lower than three years in a control group (Fernald and Gunnar, 2009). Habit change, and the gap between intent and outcome, in other words, cannot be considered distinctly from the conditions of poverty, and social protection programmes that incorporate such insights into the realm of savings, by for instance offering commitment savings products, should see multiplier effects.

More broadly, the ability to have a savings account can in turn change other behaviour, allowing families to feel secure enough in their ability to weather shocks that they might make an investment in education or in micro-enterprise they otherwise might not have made. For example, in November 2010, in an effort to test this approach, the New America Foundation's Global Assets Project helped Nigeria launch Child Development Accounts (CDAs) which provided for automatic accounts seeded with public money for approximately 1,000 junior secondary students throughout the state (New America Foundation, 2010).

Momentum

The conversion of the above trends in social protection payments across the globe has not gone unnoticed, and the result has been an undeniable building of momentum in government-to-person payments and social protection. This momentum can undoubtedly be leveraged in order to experiment more with creative social protection models, improve on current designs, consider new delivery models, and approach the problem of reaching the most vulnerable populations more creatively.

The increasing overlap between the social protection and financial inclusion fields, along with the success of both cash transfer and conditional cash transfers as highly effective elements within social protection programmes, provide a unique moment of opportunity, the G2P opportunity, for the financial services field.

As cash transfers find an increasing role in social protection pro-grammes around the globe, interest has also grown in linking social protection payments with savings accounts and opportunities. Such linkages could offer even the most poor and vulnerable populations a path to financial inclusion and asset building, in addition to their traditional human capital-enhancing objectives. Moreover, the volume of social protection payments – which can reach hundreds of millions of dollars annually – would make such accounts valuable to financial intermediaries. And, with technological advancements and expanded telecom infrastructure providing savings both to governments, in administration costs and reduced leakage, and to financial intermediaries, in operating and delivery costs, savings-linked social protection payments are an increasingly attractive option on a multitude of levels. The following section describes the savings-linked social protection concept, including where related models have been employed around the world.

The savings-linked social protection model

The concept

A savings-linked social protection model, first proposed by Zimmerman and Moury in 2009, can be defined as any social protection model that allows clients to have access to formal savings opportunities by providing them with the means to store funds electronically or in a basic bank account. Some savings-linked social protection models may go beyond merely enabling savings to explicitly rewarding it, and in certain cases making savings a requirement of the transfer. These models can come in a variety of types depending on the infrastructure available as well as the goals and target population.

We propose that such programmes can result in a number of positive outcomes: fulfilling both financial inclusion and social protection goals simultaneously; providing incentives to establish a savings habit; but also increasing the development and community effects by improving the impact and efficiency of the transfer programmes and providing formal financial vehicles.

Savings linkages can be achieved through basic transactional accounts, or low-to-no-fee and low-to-no-interest accounts which can act as a store of value for clients. That these accounts are essentially 'no frills' makes them more attractive for the financial intermediaries and more scalable, especially as branchless banking infrastructures continue to expand. We propose that such linkages can provide clients with the ability to weather shocks and invest in long-term, future-oriented outlooks and greater social empowerment.

The win–win–win: Potential results

The proposed expansion of savings-linked social protection programmes could result in positive impacts for the clients themselves, for financial intermediaries who would benefit from new accounts and capital, and for donor governments, who would improve programmes' efficiency and reduce leakage.

Individuals. Individual clients, in savings-linked social protection models, would have places to safely store and manage their money. The most poor and vulnerable populations would be able to potentially establish lines of credit, making insurance and other financial products available for the first time. Economic inclusion also, by its nature, strengthens not only community ties but also the citizen–government relationship. Additionally, since savings instruments are most often made available to female heads of households or with goals to empower women and/or their girl children, social protection models which allow savings linkages would also further encourage gender equality and empowerment across gender lines.

Financial institutions. The up-front costs for financial intermediaries of small-balance accounts have left many wary of offering accounts to the poor. The long-term benefits of the potential market, however, in light of the attractiveness of regular lump sum payments, are significant. Direct, predictable, and in many cases, significant flows of capital in the bank change the value proposition of holding savings accounts for the poorest and most vulnerable. Should clients choose to store money or save for longer-term goals in these accounts, marginal client and product costs diminish further. The potential of financial intermediaries to, eventually, bundle products such as micro-insurance and health products, in addition to microcredit, should also not be underestimated as a means to mitigate risk. If governments and international donors also contribute to investments in the necessary infrastructure, the long-term benefits to financial intermediaries could be increased further. Technological advances, as mentioned, should continue to make small balance accounts more profitable and attractive, as would a positive relationship with the government itself, which has ancillary benefits.

Governments. Developing world governments would also find savings linked protection models valuable. Traceable social protection payments will result in reduced leakage and free up more funds for other priority areas. In Liberia, as Princeton's Jonathan Friedman recently revealed, a successful shift to biometric ID-based salary payments is saving the government US$4m annually from reduced leakage. Malawi is now saving $2 m a month after shifting to e-payments. In Afghanistan, one pilot that used mobile payments to deliver salaries to police found that 10 per cent of payments had been going to non-existent policemen.

Once clients are included in the formal financial system, governments can also use these systems for other purposes such as delivering emergency aid. Eventually, these payments will not only strengthen the government–citizen relationship but also bring them into the formal sector. This should encourage a feedback loop and in turn improve other government services, as well as potentially having positive long-term effects on GDP (Barrientos and Scott, 2008).

Savings-enabling models

In its simplest form, a savings-linked social protection model enables savings behaviour by providing recipients with an effective and appropriate means to store their funds. As the shift toward electronic social protection payments increases in speed and extends geographically, such cases of incidental savings opportunities will grow in number. The varieties of programme delivery models that currently enable savings activities include:

- Accounts in a commercial bank or government post banks, such as the over 1.7 million clients of Brazil's Bolsa Família accounts; Oportunidades in Mexico, where over a million clients receive payments through accounts, as well as the Social Risk Mitigation Project in Turkey, and Colombia's Familias en Acción (Zimmerman et al., 2011).
- Retail banking agents such as those used by Mexico's Oportunidades in rural areas, in which Diconsa acts as a banking agenta for BANSEFI and Oportunidades (Ibid.).
- Prepaid debit cards or smart cards, as used in Pakistan's Benazir Income Support programme (which had a budget of roughly $38 m in 2008/2009, corresponding to the third largest public budget allocation); Jamaica's PATH programme; and Argentina's Programa Famílias (Barrientos et al., 2010).
- Mobile phones, used recently in Niger as well for NREGA in India. The Niger pilot looked at mobile versus cash payments across 116 villages in 6 communes of the Tahoua region, where 10,000 households received

$215 over a 5 month period. Mobile delivery was found to have 'strongly reduced the variable distribution costs for the implementing agency, as well as programme recipients' costs of obtaining the cash transfer' (Aker et al., 2011).

A number of programmes use more than one method of delivery.

Savings-encouraging models

Perhaps more remarkable and promising are social protection programmes or pilots in which cash transfers are not merely account-linked but which directly encourage savings behaviour through incentives or requirements. Some programmes even restrict the ways savings can be applied in order to encourage financial or human capital-building behaviour. Programme models that explicitly encourage savings include:

- Child Development Accounts (CDAs), piloted in Nigeria and Uganda, in which matching grants are given for savings and other healthy behaviours among children and youth (Meyer et al., 2009).
- Bangladesh's IGVGD programme, in which in-kind donations are given on the condition of passbook savings. A 2004 evaluation found that the mean increase in the net annual income of IGVGD beneficiary women was roughly $200, as estimated using the exchange rate at the time (Posgate et al., 2004).
- Peru's PCA or Personal Capitalization Accounts pilots, which offered matching grants to savings and financial training to clients. One PCA pilot showed that 10,000 women had saved $2 m in less than three years.
- Zambia's Kalomo Pilot Social Cash Transfer Scheme in which clients were required to open savings accounts. The programme has been resoundingly successful. As one evaluation reported, the number of beneficiary households making investments quadrupled, from about 15 to 50 per cent, and the average amount invested by clients doubled (MCDSS-GTZ, 2006).

The role of biometric identification technology in both savings-encouraging and savings-enabling social protection models should also be noted. As recently highlighted prominently in the popular press, India's Unique ID programme holds the potential to enable national financial inclusion through iris recognition technology. Kenya's Hunger Safety Net Project, too, is now employing biometrically enabled smart cards, as are other programmes such as Mexico's Oportunidades (Amin et al., 2011; United Nations Development Programme).

While they are still relatively rare, both savings-enabling and savings-encouraging programme models are increasing in number. Given the five trends shaping social protection today, there is tremendous potential to expand savings-linked programmes among the world's most vulnerable populations and to experiment with new and creative models to maximize both their efficiency and effectiveness as poverty reduction interventions. At the same time, developing and implementing the most beneficial savings-linked social protection models can be complex and should be considered in the context of a variety of challenges that need to be addressed, either on a global or a local, context-based level.

Challenges and considerations

Practical policy challenges

In implementing savings-linked social protection payments, there are a number of practical policy challenges. The cases above reveal that the appropriate models for delivering such payments vary greatly according to infrastructure, goals, and contexts.

The foremost challenge may be building the political will around the understanding of the need for financial inclusion, savings access, and asset building. Central to this process is the question of the sustainability of social protection transfers in today's economic climate. Developing-world governments are increasingly strapped for cash, and some may target relatively costly social protection payments for spending cuts. Such cuts would ignore not only the significant government savings in efficiency and effectiveness gained by shifting to e-payments, but also the apparent multiplier effects of such programmes on national economic outputs.

Within programmes, there are various ways to deliver social protection payments electronically, and the degree to which each method enables or encourages savings behaviour can vary dramatically. Taking the various contextual policy, operational, and institutional challenges into consideration will be vital in designing the most effective savings-linked social protection programmes for vulnerable populations.

There are a number of additional challenges: targeting clients who do not have proper identification; establishing seamless interoperable platforms between telecoms and banks; developing low-cost payments systems that have the potential to reach scale; and improving the financial and technological literacy issues on the beneficiary side.

While some financial institutions remain sceptical of the profitability of small-balance savings accounts, there are many ways such accounts could be beneficial for financial intermediaries, including bundling the relationship with the government, and the portfolio as a whole. Lastly, as one expert recently put it, existing 'banking regulations need to be adapted to these new possibilities of banking beyond bank branches' (Mas, 2011).

Research and implementation questions

There are specific research questions which governments, NGOs, and development experts will need to examine for savings-linked social protection payments to be optimally implemented across contexts. Relevant to the government case for such linkages, for example, are: how can the economic and social effects of programmes best be measured; how can careful impact evaluations be standardized across countries; and how can governments make the linkage of social protection payments to savings opportunities most attractive for financial intermediaries?

One important consideration, for governments wishing to implement a savings-linked social protection model, is whether at low payment levels encouraging savings might actually inhibit consumption levels. In other words: to what extent, if any, is there a trade-off between encouraging savings and increasing consumption, and at what proportion of a client's current income does it makes sense to start encouraging savings?

Another major outstanding research question that should be addressed, more broadly, is how to optimize savings-linked social protection models with complementary interventions, such as training programmes in financial literacy. Savings-linked models can also be structured to enhance the human capital components of traditional social protection programmes by linking savings to educational and health outcomes, among other variables.

In terms of stakeholder coordination, how best can the development community coordinate to help gather and test various savings-linked social protection models? In regard to regulatory issues, how are money-laundering concerns best addressed on a national and regional level? For design issues, is it preferable for programmes to at first merely enable savings, encouraging it only in later phases, or are they contexts in which explicitly encouraging savings makes immediate sense? Additionally, how can savings-linked social protection payments meet both liquidity and illiquidity needs? Should donors direct funds toward social protection schemes that are at scale, or should funds be directed to smaller programmes and more experimental savings-linked models? In which cases are commitment savings models most appropriate? And how can donors coordinate to optimize their roles in promoting financial education?

Lastly, there is the question of how governments can best contract with financial intermediaries. As Bankable Frontier Associates' David Porteous recently proposed, it may be that the optimal way for governments to contract with financial intermediaries who are delivering social protection payments is to move toward a voucher model. In such a model, governments would provide clients with vouchers, while financial intermediaries would receive some form of subsidy for each beneficiary that chooses to have funds delivered through that institution (Zimmerman et al., 2011). Such an arrangement would be likely to produce a healthy competition among banks that would be driven by the needs of the clients.

Issues for further consideration

The delivery of social protection payments is quickly evolving. Barriers and challenges remain, but none is insurmountable, and in our view the delivery of social protection payments electronically by means that enable and encourage savings is highly promising. To ensure that the transition to electronic payments is optimized for clients, donor governments, and financial intermediaries, it will be valuable to consider how to get different government ministries – such as those within the financial and social protection sectors – into productive conversations. Donors can help play a convening function here.

The role of non-profits and NGOs in helping to coordinate the evolution of savings-linked social protection models need not be limited to national coordination between ministries, however, and would be usefully extended to include regional actors and global coordination among those exploring the potential of such models. The forms of such partnerships and coordination efforts as well has how they could be standardized to order to best leverage lessons learned across contexts also require further attention.

To build on pilots and other social protection programme results, development experts can play a key role in addressing unanswered questions, driving new impact analyses and exploring potential programme models, and facilitating the appropriate coordination efforts at the regional, national, and global level. Such efforts have picked up pace over recent years, with a major colloquium on savings and social protection held in November 2010 along with an expert roundtable the following spring (Zimmerman et al., 2011). Yet in light of the potential benefits of these models, it is critically important to maximize coordination efforts at this early stage to meet the needs of the poorest.

Conclusion

The benefits of social protection payments when reaching the most vulnerable populations are now well documented. In Brazil, social protection payments resulted in increased labour participation. In Africa, payments resulted in significant reductions in sexually transmitted diseases. Social protection payments have resulted in increased immunization rates, higher consumption levels, and increased school enrolment for boys and girls. For social protection payments linked to savings opportunities, however, the potential is unfulfilled.

The poor can and do save, and have shown a real demand for financial tools to invest, to reduce weather shocks, and to smooth income. While different models are certainly appropriate for various contexts, in all programmes, linking savings opportunities to social protection payments would not only provide these tools to the most vulnerable populations, but also have a multiplier effect on the economy.

The global momentum toward cash-based social protection and savings-encouraging financial inclusion suggest that we are at a critical crossroads, presenting developing-world governments with a key opportunity to innovate at the overlap between the two fields. Of course, the relationship between financial inclusion and social protection goals, policies, and programmes is very complex, and involves an interaction of multiple stakeholders and interests. In regard to the exact role of donor agencies as well as the specifics of programme design and evaluation, there remain major questions that need to be addressed. While momentum is building, much of it remains uncoordinated, and stakeholders are still struggling with a number of difficult challenges.

To meet the need to learn more about savings-linked social protection models and opportunities will require further experimentation, topical and comparative analyses, thorough research, and facilitated coordi-nation efforts on national and regional levels. Policymakers seeking to pilot social protection programmes with savings linkages will need to consider the current state of financial inclusion, the goal of the programme, the regulatory barriers, the incentives of financial intermediaries, and the appropriate adoption of new technologies. Careful monitoring and evaluation strategies can clarify the best places for government and donor resources.

While the challenges and opportunities presented in this paper do not represent the gamut of considerations for savings-linked social protection policies and models, we believe that the evidence suggests that there is great potential for more experimentation and research. In the long term, simple linkages within social protection schemes to savings could provide an even more effective and efficient means of protecting and empowering the most vulnerable populations. These programmes' untapped potential presents, along with real challenges, a clear opportunity.

About the authors

Jamie Zimmerman (jamiezimmerman@gmail.com) is director and **Jamie Holmes** is policy analyst with the Global Assets Project at the New America Foundation.

References

Aker, J.C., Boumnijel, R., McClelland, A. and Tierney, N. (2011) *Zap it to Me: The Short-Term Impacts of a Mobile Cash Transfer Program* [website], The Center for Global Development, Washington, DC <http://www.cgdev.org/files/1425470_ file_Aker_et_al_Zap_It_to_Me_FINAL.pdf> [last accessed 23 January 2012].

Amin, A., Herbert, M., Dermish, A. and Dias, D. (2011) '"Is Grandma Ready for This?" Mexico's Move to Electronic G2P Payments' [website], developed for the Leadership Program for Financial Inclusion, Tufts University <http://fletcher. tufts.edu/CEME/publications/~/media/Fletcher/Microsites/CEME/pubs/pdfs/ Apr%2011%20Mexico%20Kills%20Cash.pdf> [last accessed 23 January 2012].

Barrientos, A. and Scott, J. (2008) 'Social transfers and growth: A review', *BWPI Working Paper* no. 52 [website], Brooks World Poverty Institute, University of Manchester, UK <http://www.bwpi.manchester.ac.uk/resources/Working-Papers/bwpi-wp-5208.pdf> [last accessed 23 January 2012].

Barrientos, A., Niño-Zarazúa, M.A. and Maitrot, M. (2010) *Social Assistance in Developing Countries Database Version 5.0* [website], Brooks World Poverty Institute, University of Manchester, UK <http://ssrn.com/abstract=1672090> [last accessed 23 January 2012].

Consultative Group to Assist the Poor (2008) Leveraging G2P Payments for Financial Inclusion [website], CGAP <http://www.cgap.org/p/site/c/template. rc/1.26.3810/> [last accessed 23 January 2012].

Fernald, L.C. and Gunnar, M.R. (2009) 'Poverty-alleviation program participation and salivary cortisol in very low-income children', *Social Science and Medicine* 68: 2180–9, http://dx.doi.org/10.1016/j.socscimed.2009.03.032

Hanlon, J., Barrientos, A. and Hulme, D. (2010) *Just Give Money to the Poor: The Development Revolution from the Global South*, Kumarian Press, Sterling, VA.

Hashemi, S.M. and de Montesquiou, A. (2011) 'Reaching the Poorest: Lessons from the Graduation Model', *Focus Note* no. 69 [website], CGAP <http://www. cgap. org/gm/document-1.9.50739/FN69.pdf> [last accessed 23 January 2012].

Jackelen, H., Zimmerman, J., Holmes, J., Sivakumaran, S. and Sobhani, S. (2011) *A Third Way for Official Development Assistance* [website], New America Foundation, Washington, DC and UNDP, New York <http://gap.newamerica. net/sites/newamerica.net/files/policydocs/AThirdWayForODA.pdf> [last accessed 23 January 2012].

Lindert, K., Linder, A., Hobbs, J. and de la Brière, B. (2007) 'The Nuts and Bolts of Brazil's Bolsa Família Program: Implementing Conditional Cash Transfers in a Decentralized Context', *SP Discussion Paper* no. 0709 [website], World Bank, Washington, DC <http://josiah.berkeley.edu/2008Fall/ARE253/ PN3%20 Services%20for%20Poor/Brazil_BolsaFamilia.pdf> [last accessed 23 January 2012].

Mas, I. (2011) 'Transforming access to finance in developing countries through mobile phones: Creating an enabling policy framework', *Banking & Finance Law Review* 27 <http://papers.ssrn.com/sol3/papers.cfm?abstract_id=1779024> [last accessed 23 January 2012].

MCDSS-GTZ *Social* Safety Net *Project* (2006) *Evaluation Report: Kalomo Social Cash Transfer Scheme [website]*, Lusaka <http://www.gtz.de/de/dokumente/ en-kalomo-scts-evaluation-report-zm.pdf> [last accessed 23 January 2012].

Meyer, J., Masa, R. and Zimmerman, J. (2009) 'Overview of child development accounts in developing countries', *Center for Social Development Working Paper* no. 09-55 [website] <http://newamerica.net/publications/policy/ overview_of_child_development_accounts_in_developing_countries> [last accessed 23 January 2012].

New America Foundation (2010) Youth Savings in Developing Countries: Trends in Practice, Gaps in Knowledge [website], New America Foundation <http://gap. newamerica.net/publications/policy/youthsave> [last accessed 23 January 2012].

Pickens, M., Porteous, D. and Rotman, S. (2009) 'Banking the Poor via G2P Payments', *Focus Note* no. 58 [website], CGAP, Washington, DC <http://www. cgap.org/gm/document-1.9.41174/FN58.pdf> [last accessed 23 January 2012].

Posgate, D., Craviolatti, P., Hossain, N., Osinski, P., Parker, T. and Sultana, P. (2004) 'Review of the BRAC/CFPR Specially Targeted Ultra-Poor (STUP) Programme: Mission Report', unpublished report, BRAC Donor Liaison Office, Dhaka.

Soares, F.V., Perez Ribas, R. and Guerreiro Osório, R. (2007) 'Evaluating the Impact of Brazil's Bolsa Família: Cash Transfer Programmes in Comparative Perspective', *IPC Evaluation Note* no. 1 [website], International Poverty Centre, Brasília, Brazil <http://www.ipc-undp.org/pub/IPCEvaluationNote1. pdf> [last accessed 23 January 2012].

Soares, S., Guerreiro Osório, R., Veras Soares, F., Medeiros, M. and Zepeda, E. (2007) 'Conditional Cash Transfers in Brazil, Chile and Mexico: Impacts upon Inequality', *Working Paper* no. 35 [website], International Poverty Center, Brasilia, Brazil <http://www.ipc-undp.org/pub/IPCWorkingPaper35.pdf> [last accessed 23 January 2012].

United Nations Development Programme, 'The Social Protection Context in Kenya' [website] <http://south-south.ipc-undp.org/about-us/item/180-the-so-cial-protection-context-in-kenya> [last accessed 23 January 2012].

World Bank (2010) *Cash Payments Can Reduce HIV/Sexually Transmitted Infections in Africa: New Bank Studies* [website], World Bank, Washington, DC <http://web.worldbank.org/WBSITE/EXTERNAL/NEWS/0,contentMDK:2265 1958~pagePK:34370~piPK:34424~theSitePK:4607,00.html> [last accessed 23 January 2012].

Zimmerman, J. and Moury, Y. (2009) *Savings-Linked Conditional Cash Transfers: A New Policy Approach to Global Poverty Reduction*, A Global Assets Project Policy Brief [website], New America Foundation, Washington, DC <http://www.newamerica.net/files/nafmigration/NAF_CCT_Savings_April09_ Final.pdf> [last accessed 23 January 2012].

Zimmerman, J. and Holmes, J. et al. with DeGiovanni, Frank , Jackelen, Henry, Sivakumaran, Subathirai, Sobhani, Sahba, McHale, Brandee, and Moury, Yves (2011) *Savings-Linked Conditional Cash Transfers: Lessons, Challenges and Directions* [website], New America Foundation, Washington, DC <http://gap.newamerica.net/sites/newamerica.net/files/program_pages/attachm ents/ SLCCTColloquiumReport.pdf> [last accessed 23 January 2012].

CHAPTER 3

Myths, misconceptions, and the emerging truth in serving very poor households: Grameen Foundation's experience to date

Kate Druschel Griffin and Malini Tolat

Abstract

In 2009, Grameen Foundation highlighted the difficulty of reaching the 1.4 billion people living below US$1.25 (purchasing power parity, PPP) per day and created a specialized team to identify and scale 'Solutions for the Poorest'. Through projects focusing on financial product development, livelihoods support, and value-chain approaches, we outline four emerging lessons learned since embarking on that programme: 1) there is the possibility of developing non-traditional business cases for serving the very poor; 2) graduation models that work for the poorest may not require cash and asset transfers if programmes can sequence the development of confidence, entrepreneurship, and other human capabilities alongside links to economic opportunities; 3) careful identification of the value chain could be a more important factor than targeting to increase the direct impact on the very poor in market system approaches; and 4) the promise of technology to bring savings to the poor probably needs to incorporate trusted people delivering on that technology.

Keywords: very poor, graduation models, microfinance, pathways out of poverty, value chains, savings

In 2009, Grameen Foundation embarked on a new strategic plan. One bold piece of that plan asked the question, 'Why has microfinance failed to serve the world's poorest households with the same scale and success as less poor households?' In an effort to address this, and to find and replicate models that might work, the Solutions for the Poorest programme was born. We began by asking two important questions: 'What are the root causes of this type of extreme poverty?' and 'Why has microfinance failed to serve this population to date?' In answering these questions, we heard some powerful myths about the lives of very poor households and the ability for social businesses such as microfinance institutions to serve them that would need to be addressed as we implemented the programme.

We recognized three key factors at play. First, microfinance still had significant service gaps in reaching very poor populations, partly because not everyone working in microfinance believed the very poor could be reached

http://dx.doi.org/10.3362/9781780448879.003

sustainably, or benefit from such services. Second, extreme poverty is highly variable and is characterized by the household's vulnerability to shocks; when very poor households are hit by crisis, the effect is more extreme and the household takes longer to recover. This is largely due to limited access to risk management tools and the lack of diversified, reliable income streams. Third, some programmes that have tried to target this population have shown that very poor households can take advantage of both business opportunities and risk management financial tools when provided in an appropriate manner.

Thus we settled on a strategy that would seek to identify, test, and scale reliable, customized solutions that achieve three simultaneous objectives:

- Effectively target very poor households using rigorous methodologies.
- Address the vulnerability and volatility of their lives by focusing on financial services that mitigate risk and introducing more reliable income-generating streams that help to smooth cash flows.
- Scale these solutions as part of a core sustainable social business.

It is this last piece – the focus on serving very poor households as a core part of the strategy of a double bottom-line social business – that has proven the elusive Holy Grail for the microfinance and overall development industry.

Over the last three years, we have implemented a range of programmes that address financial product development and/or livelihoods for the poor and poorest households we hope to reach. These have focused on financial product development – introducing financial services that help to mitigate risk or blows to the household, as well as livelihoods development – introducing sustainable, reliable income-generating activities for the poorest households. In this article we refer to multiple projects within these focus areas, details of which can be found on our website at http://www.grameenfoundation.org/ what-we-do/microfinance.

In the remainder of this paper we present some myths and misconceptions that we heard as we started this work regarding working with the poorest households. For each, we have presented project experiences that either disprove the myth or present a more nuanced view of the issues.

Tackling myths and misconceptions: The emerging truth

In implementing the above-mentioned projects, we have learned a great deal about practical, scalable ways to serve very poor households as part of a sustainable social business model. The four statements we heard consistently in 2009, and against which we now have practical experiences to share, are:

- 'There is no business case for serving the very poor'.
- 'Serving the very poor requires a graduation model that starts with cash and requires asset grants'.
- 'Targeting is the best approach for integrating very poor people into market-based systems'.

- 'Technology is the critical path to reaching very poor people, particularly with savings accounts'.

For the first two statements, our experiences led us to refute the basic assumptions, whereas with the last two statements we developed a more nuanced view to the standard approach.

There is no business case for serving the very poor

The question arose early in our strategy-setting process: is there really no business case for a microfinance institution, social business, or any other institutional entity to serve the very poor, as many believe? Or, is a model of cross-subsidization required? To what extent will the poorest be able to contribute to the bottom line, or do they remain a loss-leader serviced to achieve social goals, with limited expectation of a financial return on investment?

We have been exploring this question as a component of all the projects we are implementing that require the ongoing existence of a sustainable business entity. Early learning emerged in an analysis of the operations of a partner micro-franchise institution incubated by Grameen Foundation in Indonesia. PT Rekan Usaha Mikro Anda (RUMA) is a for-profit social enterprise that was founded in 2009 with the mission of empowering poor people through mobile technology and micro-franchise. RUMA's social mission is rooted in its business model. Its social charter requires RUMA to work with clients who have an 80 per cent likelihood of being poor (defined as living on less than US$2.50 a day) and a 15 per cent likelihood of being very poor (those living on less than $1.25 a day) when starting the business, business before it can pay dividends to shareholders (see Box 3.1).

RUMA offers a business-in-a-box solution that is specifically targeted to underserved communities and provides them with the support needed to be successful entrepreneurs. The business is designed to facilitate the sale of products based on mobile technology; products ranging from airtime to a mobile-based job site.

In 2010 (after one year of operation) RUMA had reached approximately 3,500 clients, and Grameen Foundation leveraged the rich data RUMA had collected on the business operations and poverty levels of its clients to explore the performance levels of different poverty segments. The expectation from the data-analysis project was that it would validate the basic assumptions RUMA had used to model its growth strategy, including the expectation that the very poor client segment would probably demonstrate higher dropout rates, transact at lower rates, and generate proportionately less revenue for RUMA. These assumptions were reflected in the ground operations as RUMA's field staff limited their recruitment of very poor micro-entrepreneurs to achieve their minimum targets, but, beyond that, focused energies on recruitment of less poor entrepreneurs who would be expected to deliver greater revenue growth and profitability.

Box 3.1 Using the PPI

RUMA relies on the Progress out of Poverty Index® (PPI®) to measure the poverty level of potential and existing clients. The PPI uses 10 simple indicators that field workers can quickly collect and verify. Scores can be computed by hand on paper in real time. The PPI score can then be matched against various poverty likelihood tables to show the probability of a given household falling below a particular poverty line.

When RUMA and Grameen Foundation examined the actual data, the results revealed some surprising patterns in the performance of the poor and the poorest clients. Major findings were that:

- The data found no correlation between PPI level and activity level, meaning that poverty level did not automatically predict ability to run the business successfully. The poorest entrepreneurs' businesses were just as active as those of the less poor entrepreneurs. Although it was harder for them to enter the business, once they had engaged they were as capable as the less poor customer segment.
- The dropout rates were quite high in this business, but there was no significant difference in the percentage of dropouts for different poverty segments. The dropout rates were, in fact, more significantly correlated to the initial capital invested in the business and the transaction activity in the first two weeks of running the business. Surprisingly, neither one of these variables was directly correlated to PPI scores.

RUMA expected the activity level to follow the arrow in Figure 3.1; as the PPI score rose, so would the transactions. The majority of transactions did not follow any pattern.

These findings had significant implications for RUMA's growth strategy. It was clear that while recruiting and servicing the poorest entrepreneurs may be more

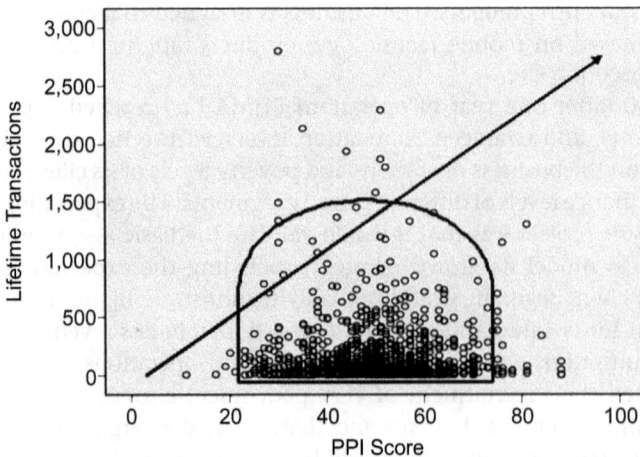

Figure 3.1 Numbers of transactions against poverty score

expensive for RUMA (segregated costing data is not yet available to determine to what extent this is the case), the net impact from the higher-than-expected revenue could ultimately lead to a positive return on investment even for RUMA's business related to the poorest customer, because their revenue contribution was at the same level as entrepreneurs that were less poor. RUMA is now assessing the possibility of adapting its strategy to recruit more entrepreneurs falling into the very poor category, thus more effectively achieving its social mission. It has since pilot tested a financing product to overcome the lack of start-up finance that limits the entry of a greater number of micro-entrepreneurs from the poorest poverty segment. It is important to point out that these findings must take into consideration that the nature of the products sold by RUMA's micro-entrepreneurs – for example mobile airtime – are products that have regular, naturally occurring, customer demand and do not require sophisticated sales acumen. The potential of the poorest to contribute to the business model is therefore dependent on the design and characteristic of the core product as well as the support and delivery mechanisms used to engage them.

Besides the micro-franchise model, we have also examined micro-finance business models that have expanded to serve poorer clientele than traditional mainstream models to test whether there is a business case for this target group. One example we have analysed is the microfinance institution Fonkoze, based in Haiti. Fonkoze has built a stair-step, or ladder, approach to serving Haiti's poor and poorest households. At the very bottom is an 18-month programme that services the poorest households which replicates BRAC's ultra-poor graduation model, called Chemin Lavi Mayo or Pathways out of Poverty. At the next step is a programme called 'Ti Kredi' which is a six-month programme that provides very short-term, very small loans that progressively get larger and longer over the six months. This essentially acts as an 'on boarding' system into the mainstream microfinance programme (the third step in the ladder) and helps clients traditionally not eligible for that programme to develop the business acumen, confidence, and lending and savings history to be eligible for the traditional solidarity group model. The third step is the solidarity group-lending model while the fourth is a small business loan for Fonkoze's most mature business women.

Analysis was conducted on the Ti Kredi programme to understand both the social and financial business case it presents to the organization (Sivalingam et al., 2012). There are clear social benefits, but the interesting analysis is whether, financially, the programme contributes to Fonkoze's double bottom line. The six-month programme costs $38 per client to implement, net of any (small) earned revenue from the interest on loans received – and if the client graduates into the solidarity lending programme after six months, all things being equal, she generates as much revenue as any other solidarity loan client. Over a three-year period, however, 61 per cent of Ti Kredi clients in our sample who had graduated into solidarity remained with the programme, compared with only 42.9 per cent of clients who had started with the solidarity programme. Ti Kredi clients who graduate stay with Fonkoze longer, allowing Fonkoze to earn a greater amount of revenue from them in the long term.

In addition, Fonkoze views the $38 cost per client as a similar fee to its normal customer-acquisition costs for the solidarity group-lending programme. For this $38 fee, they are cultivating clients who have a longer-term profitability for the institution. In this case, then, it is not a model of cross-subsidization that makes business sense, but rather a model of customer loyalty, greater retention, and customer acquisition costing.

Serving the very poor requires a graduation model that starts with cash stipends and requires asset grants

In 2009, CGAP and Ford Foundation had just embarked on an ambitious pilot to replicate the BRAC method of serving 'ultra-poor' households. This method rigorously targets and selects the poorest households in a community to participate. From there, households usually have access to a cash stipend to overcome chronic food insecurity and help with consumption support, and the programme organizes households to start saving and provides training and other support to enable the household to begin implementing a business venture such as rearing livestock. Finally, the household is given the asset (as a grant) in order to implement the livelihood activity. Throughout the process, regular mentoring and coaching is provided by programme staff and, in many locations, the community is mobilized to support the households in their journey (more information can be found at http://graduation.cgap.org).

These approaches have now been replicated in eight places around the world, and have influenced the way the microfinance and enterprise development communities have approached serving very poor households in recent years. The programmes are aiming to be more successful versions of government-provided the social safety net programmes, however, which influences the thinking around scale and sustainability of these models. Fonkoze's replication of this approach costs upwards of $1,900 per person to deliver in the 18-month timeframe; for programmes in India that cost can be as low as $330 for a 24-month programme (Hashemi and de Montesquiou, 2011). For a social business, these are costs that make it difficult to make a sound business case – even when the social results of the programme are extraordinarily compelling.

Grameen Foundation, in partnership with The Livelihood School – a part of the BASIX group of companies – is piloting a variation of this method which seeks to serve households living at the same level of poverty, but without the cash stipends and asset transfers required in the BRAC replications. Many of the same tenets apply: rigorous targeting, extensive livelihoods training, ongoing coaching and mentoring, and the involvement of the community through the use of community resource people to ensure the household's success. The activities were sequenced such that supplemental income-generating activities begin early in the process, however – within the first six months – to provide the 'consumption support' needed to help these households overturn the cash-deficit situation of their families. These are activities that are easy to implement, have low barriers to entry, and require low to no investment – usually piecemeal labour that can easily be done in the home for a few hours a day. For example, *agarbatti*, or incense-stick rolling, was introduced as a livelihood activity in the pilot in the Gaya district of the northern Indian state of Bihar. *Agarbatti* rolling brings, on average, an additional Rs.300 (= approximately $6) per month to the household

Unitus Impact programmes have also explored the viability and potential for impact on very poor households through a series of pilots with different institutions. Their learning has been surprisingly similar to the issues we have been discussing, especially the potential for a business case as well as the possibility of implementing the programme without a cash subsidy. Some key findings recently highlighted (Shenoy 2011) include:

- The realization that a well-structured 'patient' loan is more effective than an asset transfer, even for the poorest, as it increases commitment to the activity for which the loan is being used.
- It is critical to introduce a livelihood activity at the earliest stage of the project (Unitus uses the term 'Livelihoods First'). The value of additional support services such as health and confidence-building measures will not be realized unless their most critical concern – generating income to survive – is also addressed. A programme that prioritizes livelihoods first has a better chance of gaining the trust of the community, getting community members to see the value of engaging with the programme, and securing time commitments to other more qualitative inputs that will provide longer-term benefits, thus providing a platform for greater sustainability.

Grameen Foundation and Unitus's experiences are not, in themselves, contrary to the widely-held belief that savings or a cash stipend are the entry level intervention for very poor households. Our experiences suggest, however, that a more detailed breakdown of the steps needed to instil commitment to the project and minimum capability can include introducing wage labour as a substitute for the cash transfer, which can parallel the introduction of savings services. Savings still remains the first 'financial' intervention, but link to a livelihood activity early in the programme; this approach serves to overcome the initial barriers to participation faced when attempting to engage cash-deficit households into structured programming. Building from this point, households can then move into more entrepreneurial activities financed by a tailored credit product in lieu of an asset transfer.

Targeting is the best approach for integrating very poor people into market-based systems

Market system-based approaches have become a widespread strategy for achieving large-scale impact for poor populations. These approaches, termed broadly as 'Making Markets Work for the Poor' (DFID) or 'Value Chain Approach' (USAID), have seen significant success in turning the dial on poverty reduction efforts. These approaches have struggled to demonstrate direct or indirect benefits for very poor populations, and there is considerable discussion amongst pro-poor practitioners on the way to achieve greater success in this area. Often, projects with specific objectives to be inclusive of very poor populations will prioritize geographic and individual targeting to ensure the inclusion of the poorest. Others have assumed that these approaches can directly benefit only the more capable within the bottom of the pyramid, while creating trickle-down benefits to the poorest. None of these points of view is yet to be fully substantiated owing to lack of adequate data.

> Projects have assumed that vulnerable populations will benefit from wealth creation within the community even when they are not direct participants. This assumption has rarely been backed with analysis to understand how intra-household and inter-household resource transfers function within a specific context, and thus this trickle-down effect has rarely been confirmed (USAID microlinks).

As Grameen Foundation explored the challenges associated with integrating the very poor into market-based projects through a series of value-chain development projects carried out in India, Uganda, and Mali, we found that, while targeting is an important function of ensuring that the poor will be integrated and receive project benefits, it may be much more relevant to focus on the initial selection of the value chain, the process for analysis during value-chain selection, and resultant design of the intervention, to ensure greater, sustainable impact. In short, it may not be a lack of directed attention during implementation, but the systemic process that is used to select the value chain and conceptualize the project that may provide the most meaningful benefits. These benefits may include not only greater inclusion of the poorest but also greater probability of their benefiting directly from project interventions.

As an example, in India we partnered with Access Development Services to identify value chain opportunities. Initially, a standard approach to value-chain selection was followed, which included identifying opportunities in disproportionately poor geographies and those that specifically engaged large numbers of poor households. Through this process, the peanut value chain in West Bengal made the shortlist as a good opportunity for a project that included the poorest. A subsequent, more systematic selection process came up with two completely different value chains: sericulture (silk) in West Bengal and maize in Rajasthan. That the results included sericulture was particularly surprising as it would not have made the shortlist using the original process. While all the identified value chains were prevalent in poor geographies and engaged large numbers of poor people, the two selected by the more refined process engaged larger numbers of the poorest households in activities that could be meaningfully upgraded and linked to markets. There was also less risk attached to facilitating the interventions for the poorest households in these value chains (a critical factor to be taken into consideration when designing any programme for the poorest).

This adapted process compared multiple value chains within the same poor geographies but focused on identifying specific risks and opportunities for clearly segmented population groups (i.e. the poor at below $2.50 per day and the poorest at below $1.25 per day). Grameen Foundation's Progress out of Poverty Index (PPI)® was used during the field study and subsequently analysed the participant responses based on their poverty levels. The factors we explored included:

- participation level within the value chain of the poor and poorest categories;
- nature of activities within the value chain based on poverty level;
- challenges and bottlenecks segmented by poverty level;
- risks and opportunities of different interventions by poverty segment.

The consideration of market factors and impact potential on the poor more broadly should continue to be a significant variable. Segmenting the potential constraints and opportunities that can be achieved through selected interventions aimed at the poorest, however, is essential for the sustainability of these efforts. In fact, some of the interventions that are the most appropriate for the poorest can emerge from more broad-based efforts to develop the value chain for the less poor, such as service opportunities within the value chain. For example, demand for mechanized post-harvest processing services for maize in Northern Uganda led to the creation of an agribusiness that provides these services on-farm using a mobile unit that employs five people per unit during the harvest season.

Table 3.1 provides an example of this approach, looking at two value chains in West Bengal. While the *biri* industry (local version of cigarettes based on *tendu* leaves) engaged the largest number of the poorest, sericulture had greater scope for increasing income and growth opportunities.

Technology is the critical path to reaching very poor people, particularly with savings accounts

Several years ago, savings and technology simultaneously rose in popularity among the microfinance community. The Bill & Melinda Gates Foundation had made savings a major part of their Financial Services for the Poor strategy, and several other donors were stressing the importance of providing savings services to a population that had been inundated with microcredit products. Proponents of group-based savings groups (self-help groups, village savings and loan associations, rotating savings and credit associations, etc.) promoted these programmes as the best methods of reaching the very poor. At the same time, buzzwords such as 'branchless banking' started appearing. M-Pesa began its meteoric rise to claim majority market share for mobile money in Kenya, sparking a worldwide hunt for the next great M-Pesa replicator that would change the way financial services are delivered to poor households around the world. Three years later, we have our own experiences with implementing savings products for the poor and poorest, but also with the use of technology

Table 3.1 Value chain comparison matrix

Criteria	Biri	Sericulture
Engagement of poorest households	More than 1 million poor households, in most of the blocks in the district	Concentrated in four/five blocks Approximately 50,000 plus households,
Mode of engagement	As labour only (there are selected blocks where more than 90% of the poorest households are engaged in *biri*)	In multiple ways: mulberry producer, cocoon producer, reeler, weaver etc. (5% as agri labourer, 30% as mulberry and yarn producer, and 65% as weavers)
New opportunities for the poorest at different levels of value chain	Limited scope for new opportunities beyond acting as middle-man	Good possibility for diversifying existing activities to mulberry production, cocoon rearing, spinning, and yarn trading. Also transportation to directly link silk producers and weavers
Potential of greater value transfer to poorest households	Economic value: limited potential of enhancing existing rates for *biri* rolling. Social value for engagement is high to improve basic conditions and introduce better processes to manage the negative health effects of the activities	Scope for increasing income by at least 80% for existing activity in weaving. Income expansion for new activities in mulberry production will generate additional income to diversify existing cash flows

mobile money in in reaching these households. Moreover, through the use of Grameen Kenya Foundation's PPI®, the data exists to see how people at different poverty levels are saving.

As a start, the current poverty outreach of the three MFIs we're working with is shown in Table 3.2.

So far, Grameen Foundation has the best data for CARD Bank, where the least poor of the savings clients have an average balance of $74 while the poorest have a balance of $37 – a difference to be sure, but the poorest are still saving in the accounts. At CASHPOR, where the poorest customers are being served by the three pilots, a savings product through ICICI Bank is being piloted (owing to Indian regulations, CASHPOR acts as a banking correspondent), and

Table 3.2 Poverty outreach data

	CARD Bank %	CASHPOR %	ACSI%
$1.25/day PPP	19.71	75.2	25
$2.50/day PPP	50.34	96.2	79

Note: In comparison, the number of people in the Philippines living below $1.25/ day PPP is 18.2 per cent and 47.5 per cent for under $2.50/day PPP. For India, the percentage of the population under $1.25/ day PPP is 42.6 per cent and 74.9 per cent for under $2.50/day. Both CARD and CASHPOR are reaching poor populations in excess of those found in the national population.

in eight months CASHPOR has already opened over 42,000 accounts with an average balance of $2.82.

At our pilot in Bihar, India, mentioned above, where the poorest clients among all our programmes are being served, households have been organized into 'adapted' self-help groups to facilitate savings mobilization ('adapted' because they are smaller than the usual SHGs organized in India and have a deeper focus on livelihood promotion). While it took some time to organize the groups because the households were resistant to the usefulness of such groups (which was mitigated through exposure visits and learning conversations with other similar women in their communities successfully operating SHGs), the majority of households have committed to saving Rs.20 per month (approximately $0.50); from June 2011 through January 2012, a total of $340 was saved by 133 households – an average of $2.55 per person.

Clearly, the very poorest households are able to commit to savings and have demand for such products. The role technology can play in making that happen, however, is perhaps the more interesting story. In the market research across all three countries, customers stated convenience and accessibility as key attributes they were looking for in a savings account. They did not seem to mistrust mobile phones or ATMs as ways to save. In practice, however, the human face accompanying the technology is key to making those transactions happen. At CASHPOR, where our technology partner Eko ensures that the transaction can be done entirely on the customer's mobile phone – and the CASHPOR field agent serves as the cash in/cash out point customers hand over their phones, their PIN numbers, and their deposit to the field agent. They trust that their CASHPOR agent – who they see on a weekly basis – will conduct the transaction for them, and they do not need to be involved any further in the process. Where there was initial resistance to opening the accounts in the first place, however (mobile phones were seen as the toys of the young, and it would be disreputable for a married, middle-aged woman like a CASHPOR client to transact on one), this quickly dissipated once a few women had signed up and started transacting, and a domino effect of account opening began. At CARD Bank, where ATMs were installed, in the first months after opening nearly 100 per cent of withdrawals were accompanied by a balance inquiry – but that figure has declined to about 70 per cent in the intervening eight months. This could mean clients trust the device more and/or are more adept at remembering their balances before making a withdrawal.

So, we can validate the importance of savings and the demand for safe, flexible, convenient accounts from even the poorest of households. Technology can also be a key component to increasing accessibility and convenience of accounts, but adoption by clients will continue to need a human touch in order to occur. Trusted intermediaries will help to build confidence in using the technology, in ensuring customers understand safety and security measures designed to protect them, and building uptake for the poorest households. People, in fact, remain the critical path to reaching the poorest, with technology in an important supporting role.

Conclusion

In just over two years of implementing projects meant to provide risk-management tools and income-generating opportunities to the world's poor and poorest households, we have begun to see some interesting lessons emerge that will help guide us in future programming. We now believe that:

- It is possible to find a business case for working with the very poor. It may require some innovative thinking – and it will definitely require a great deal of data – but the very poorest households can actually contribute in interesting ways to both sides of the double bottom line. Cross-subsidization is not the only answer, although it is one piece of the puzzle.
- The very poorest households will need a lot more hand-holding, training, and mentoring to help them on their journey out of poverty. We are starting to see, however, that it may be possible to achieve that graduation effect without the need for major cash subsidies and asset transfers as long as the personal touch is effectively implemented. The most important part of moving beyond these cash subsidies and asset transfers is meeting the income-generating needs of these households early on, through easy-implement means.
- Market-system approaches must make a concerted effort to clearly segment the voices of the poorest in each step of the value chain analysis. Without this, such market system approaches may miss important opportunities to sustainably change these markets to better work for the poorest households.
- Savings is a crucial product for the world's poorest households – and one they eagerly will take up regardless of the absence or presence of technology. Technology, however, will not fulfil its promise on delivering savings services to the very poorest households unless we value the role of trusted intermediaries – the human face that accompanies the delivery of the service and builds trust in that system. It will take time for one to replace the other, and may never reach that point for the very poorest and most vulnerable households.

About the authors

Kate Druschel Griffin is Director and **Malini Tolat** (mtolat@grameenfoundation.org) is Programme Manager at the Solutions for the Poorest Department of the Grameen Foundation

References

Hashemi, S. and de Montesquiou, A. (2011) 'Reaching the poorest: Lessons from the graduation model', *CGAP Focus Note* No. 69, CGAP, Washington, DC.

Shenoy, S.(2011) *The Ultra Poor Program: An Examination of Livelihoods*, Partners in Prosperity Case Study 2009-2011, Seattle, Unitus;New Delhi, Partners in Prosperity.

Sivalingam, L., Slocum, B. and Druschel Griffin, K. (2012) *A Double Bottom Line Business Case for Serving Very Poor Households,* Grameen Foundation, Washington, DC <http://www.grameenfoundation.org/double-bottom-line-business-case-serving-very-poor-households>

USAID microlinks. (n.d.) 'V. Vulnerable populations and the value chain approach' <http://microlinks.kdid.org/good-practice-center/value-chain-wiki/vulnerable-populations-and-value-chain-approach> [accessed 18 June 2012].

CHAPTER 4

Inclusive microfinance: reaching disabled people through partnership development

Anne Leymat

Abstract

This study examines projects that support access to financial services for disabled people, highlighting good practices that guarantee efficiency and sustainability of initiatives with a particular focus on the use of microcredit. The study is based on the findings of: a global survey and interviews with disabled people's organizations and microfinance providers; a literature review; field studies in seven countries; and the outcome of two regional workshops (in Kenya and Bangladesh) and a practitioner workshop in Geneva. It is estimated that 10 to 12 per cent of the world's population has some kind of impairment and of those around 82 per cent live below the poverty line. Most people with impairments who work are self-employed. However, access to financial services for disabled people remains sporadic. The central part of the study explores the potential for successful, responsible, and complementary partnership development between microfinance actors and disabled people's organizations. Our findings demonstrate that if disabled people are given the opportunity to access financial services, many are capable of successfully managing loans and businesses – thereby becoming agents of their own development.

Keywords: disability, microfinance, empowerment

Disabled people represent 15 per cent of the world's population, equating to 470 million people of working age (WHO/World Bank, 2011). The vast majority of disabled people, if given the opportunity, can contribute to the economic development of their communities. However, 82 per cent of disabled people live below the poverty line. Indeed, poverty is considered both a cause and a consequence of disability (DFID, 2000). Poverty is a *cause* of disability because the poor often have difficult living conditions (for example hazardous housing and working conditions), a lack of resources to prevent malnutrition, and a lack of access to adequate health services, all of which can lead to serious health conditions and impairments. Poverty is a *consequence* of disability because disabled people often lack access to education, health services, and income-generating activities; they are often denied their human, social, and economic rights. These factors contribute to high levels of vulnerability and exclusion. Being able to earn a stable income is therefore a main priority for disabled people.

http://dx.doi.org/10.3362/9781780448879.004

Like the rest of the population in developing economies, most economically active disabled people (around 80 per cent) turn to self-employment because of a lack of opportunities in the formal job market. While most people would prefer to have a job with regular income, self-employment is often the only option available. For example, many disabled people have started shops or craft workshops; others are involved in street vending, tailoring, carpentry, etc. In rural areas, self-employment also includes farming or agricultural activities. The majority of disabled people in developing countries live in rural areas, like the rest of the population.

Like any entrepreneur, disabled people often need access to microfinance services, in particular microcredit, to develop their business. However, very few disabled people have access to microfinance services. Disabled people have different types of impairment; they also have diverse combinations of education and skills. As such, activities for financial inclusion need to be flexible to respond to individual needs and interests.

The human rights approach to disability aims at guaranteeing equal rights and opportunities for disabled people. In the context of self-employment, this means that disabled people should have the possibilities for accessing the same financial services from mainstream providers as the rest of the population. The United Nations Convention on the Rights of Persons with Disabilities (CRPD), adopted in 2006, addresses this directly. Indeed, CRPD article 27 asserts disabled people's rights to decent work and to gain a living.

Objective of the research

Handicap International decided to carry out an international study on access to funding mechanisms, loans, and grants for disabled people, with the overall goal of producing a framework document to highlight good practices on the use of financial services. More specifically, the objectives were to:

- raise awareness on the rights and capacities of disabled people to access affordable and sustainable financial services;
- share approaches and methodologies on how to facilitate access to funding mechanisms through partnership development;
- illustrate good practices and lessons learned in various contexts through practical examples;
- suggest a series of guidelines and practical recommendations on how microfinance providers can reach out to a significant potential clientele of disabled people, and be more inclusive towards disabled people.

Thus, one of the overall objectives of this study was to identify strategies that help reduce poverty among disabled people, in this case through access to microcredit for self-employment.

This paper summarizes the main content of the Good Practices publication.

Research methodology

This study was carried out by Handicap International and financed by the Swiss Agency for Development and Cooperation.

It was conducted in three main phases: *Phase one* consisted of a literature review and the collection of information through desk studies and research on financial inclusion projects that have involved or currently involve disabled people. We identified a number of sources to examine the major issue on outreach to vulnerable populations. These included: reports by organizations of/for disabled people, local and international NGOs, United Nations, and development agencies; books and handbooks on good practices for microfinance published by mainstream microfinance institutions, United Nations Capital Development Fund (UNCDF), and the Consultative Group to Assist the Poor (CGAP). We analysed available information on microfinance for disabled people, although literature on this topic is generally scarce. This phase also included a survey sent to local and international microfinance providers and organizations of/for disabled people around the world. A total of 463 organizations were contacted for this study; 107 responded – 57 were organizations of/for disabled people and 50 were specialized microfinance providers (these included local NGOs, international NGOs, and microfinance institutions). The survey questionnaire included details on methodologies, institutional features, credit policies, challenges, and achievements.

Having conducted a broad research of current practices to access funding mechanisms, the next step for phase one was to identify some particularly interesting and innovative programmes for field visits. Phase one led to the selection of programmes from a variety of regions which had been particularly successful. Criteria for choosing locations for field visits included: use of innovative approaches, stability of the programmes and implementing organizations, number of members/beneficiaries/borrowers/ clients, and number of programmes in a single country/region.

The goal of *Phase two* was to compare field practices and deepen the analysis of specific organizations. To do so, the research team conducted field trips to India, Bangladesh, Afghanistan, Kenya, Ethiopia, and Nicaragua to meet with disabled people, organizations of/for disabled people and microfinance providers that had succeeded in providing funding mechanisms for disabled people. This phase also consisted of the organization of two regional workshops, in Bangladesh and Kenya, in which 17 organizations gathered to exchange their concrete experiences and good practices.

Phase three consisted of the drafting of a good practices handbook on the basis of the information collected and the outcome of the field visits and workshops. A first draft was reviewed by microfinance experts, grants providers, and organizations of/for disabled people as part of a two-day workshop organized in Geneva, Switzerland.

Challenges and possible biases

A first challenge with the literature review was that very little research has been done on access to funding mechanisms for disabled people. The research team tried to target more general programmes for *vulnerable populations* and also to focus on one of the main debates in microfinance today, which is particularly relevant for our topic: whether financial sustainability and outreach to the poor are compatible; and the roles of the different stakeholders. Another challenge was reaching a sufficient number of organizations through the survey, as we received fewer responses than expected. This may be indicative of a widespread lack of experience of providing funding mechanisms for disabled people, but also perhaps a lack of interest in the topic. Indeed, several mainstream microfinance institutions and development agencies answered openly that disabled people were not their target population. Other microfinance institutions informed us that it was difficult to know the extent to which they served disabled people as this was not a variable that they recorded. Therefore, some of these experiences reported were based on anecdotes. The research team would like to emphasize that this is not an exhaustive overview of the initiatives that exist worldwide.

Main research findings

Low representation of disabled people in microfinance

A major finding of the study was that disabled people are highly under-represented among the clients of microfinance institutions. Of the 50 microfinance providers that responded to the survey, only 27 had significant experience of working with disabled people. Microfinance organizations reported that 0–0.5 per cent of their clients are disabled people. However, this number should be treated with caution, as some institutions said it was impossible for them to know how many disabled people they have served, as this is not one of their control variables, and this would depend on the definition of disability. All specialized microfinance providers affirmed they do not discriminate against disabled people. However, many microfinance institutions (including large, well-respected institutions) responded that disabled people are not their target population.

Main barriers to financial inclusion

Two main kinds of barrier to financial inclusion were identified:

1. *'Internal' barriers* (directly linked with disabled people), which include factors such as lack of business skills, lack of formal education, lack of self-confidence, or lack of access to information. This also relates to self-exclusion, where people choose not to access microfinance, which is usually the result of a lack of self-confidence and knowledge about how such services can be beneficial. This may be a particular problem

for disabled people, who often experience a considerable level of social exclusion and rejection, which affects their decisions regarding services such as financial provision. Another type of self-exclusion is the expectation of some disabled people and their families to rely on charity as a means of income. This attitude is incompatible with sustainable microfinance institutions and will naturally lead to exclusion of such potential clients.

2. *'External' barriers*, which refer both to stigma and prejudice in the social environment and to inaccessible microfinance institutions. For the latter, examples would include: inadequate financial product design (where microfinance institutions require applicants to have prior professional experience of 6 months before being eligible for a credit); a lack of accessibility (to both physical premises and information/communication resources); and/or attitudinal barriers (stigmas and prejudices) by microfinance institution staff and other members in solidarity groups and village banking. Owing to attitudes and prejudices in society, staff of microfinance institutions often deliberately or unconsciously exclude disabled people. Such staff often lack the necessary experience and training to estimate the real resource base and to distinguish the difference between real credit risk and perceived credit risk when it comes to disabled people. If a microfinance institution practises any form of group methodology there is also evidence that 'staff pressure' triggers the 'peer pressure' leading to exclusion of poorer members.

An interesting result of the research is that organizations of/for disabled people and microfinance institutions do not identify the same barriers for disabled people:

* Most of the organizations of/for disabled people affirmed that for disabled people, lack of education, low income, stigmatization, and lack of access to information are the most serious barriers to financial inclusion.
* Most microfinance institutions think that for disabled people, lack of self-esteem, lack of guarantees/collateral, and lack of access to information are the most serious barriers.

Promising approaches to financial inclusion

In response to the low representation of disabled people in microfinance institutions, two main approaches are used: 1) inclusion in mainstream microfinance institutions; or 2) provision of financial services by organizations of/for disabled people themselves. A major finding of this research is that the most cost-efficient and sustainable way of providing financial services for disabled people is to facilitate their access to mainstream financial provision.

The following sections discuss the two approaches and highlight good practices that have been identified throughout the research.

Inclusion in mainstream microfinance institutions

This is achieved through a variety of approaches, including: 1) raising aware-ness among microfinance staff; 2) establishing partnerships for cooperation between organizations of/for disabled people and microfinance institutions; 3) promoting reasonable accommodation: adapting methodologies, product design, and accessibility; or 4) simply by supporting disabled people to submit their loan applications.

Raising awareness among microfinance staff

The staff of microfinance institutions, and particularly the credit officers, are a core target group to influence as a means to increase outreach to disabled people. However, if such influence is to be efficient, it should be backed by senior management of the microfinance institution. For example, in order to reduce discrimination and exclusion on the part of microfinance institution staff, some organizations, such as AMFIU (Association of Microfinance Institutions of Uganda), organized seminars within their own organization to raise awareness on disability issues and on the rights of disabled people. For this training, topics included:

- Training loan officers on how to make an objective risk analysis that does not discriminate against disabled people.
- Discuss stigmatization and prejudice with loan officers, managers, own-ers, etc. If top-level managers have a commitment towards disability is-sues and inclusion, this is often filtered down throughout the rest of the institution.
- Publicize 'success stories' to raise awareness of the potential of disabled entrepreneurs within microfinance institutions and society as a whole.

Establishing partnerships for cooperation between organizations of/for disabled people and microfinance institutions

The research identified examples of good practices in terms of cooperation between microfinance institutions and disabled people's organizations. For example, the Ethiopian Federation for Persons with Disabilities (EFPD) established an agreement with a microfinance institution, GASHA, with the main objective of developing entrepreneurship among disabled women by providing business skills and vocational training, and micro-finance and business development services. The methodology used was as follows: EFPD subsidized half of the interest rate to facilitate access for disabled people to financial services. It also covered half of the obligatory savings, which had been found to be an obstacle for disabled people wishing to apply for loans.

Another example would be AMFIU and the National Union of Disabled Persons in Uganda (NUDIPU), which launched a pilot project in 2005, 'The

Microfinance and Disability Project', with support from the Norwegian Association of the Disabled. The project goals were:

- to raise awareness among microfinance institutions about the largely unexploited market for financial services among disabled people;
- to raise awareness among organizations of disabled people, and eliminate fear and misconceptions regarding microfinance institutions; to promote the idea among vulnerable disabled people that they do not need 'charity' and are expected to repay a loan, as other people do.

To achieve these goals, activities included:

- Organizing a two-day workshop for organizations of/for disabled people and microfinance institutions. The workshop created a positive attitude among participants and showcased successful examples of disabled entrepreneurs.
- Creating an award for the most 'disability-friendly' microfinance institution.
- Implementing a survey among AMFIU members to find out the proportion of disabled people among their clients and to analyse their knowledge and experience on equalization of opportunities for disabled people.

Both organizations have employed a specific project officer to manage this project: the AMFIU disability officer raised awareness among microfinance institutions on disability issues; the NUDIPU microfinance officer met disabled people, offered advice and training on business skills, and tried to raise confidence in their business capacities.

Reasonable accommodation: adapting methodologies, financial product design, and accessibility

Interestingly, 70 per cent of the microfinance providers that provide loans to disabled people stated they had done so under the same conditions as the rest of their clients. Many of them highlighted the fact that disabled people were among their best clients, demonstrating that they may be as reliable businessmen and businesswomen as the rest of the population.

Finally, about a quarter of the microfinance providers that have served disabled people reported that they used some kind of special arrangement, including lowering market interest rate (five institutions, 20 per cent) and longer repayment terms (two institutions, 3.5 per cent). Several institutions also reported having made physical accessibility arrangements for their premises.

The credit methodology utilized by microfinance institutions can prevent the participation of disabled people (as well as other marginalized groups). For example, because of mobility difficulties or inaccessible transport, a weekly repayment frequency might be a higher obstacle for a disabled person than for a non-disabled person. This may especially be the case during the initial stages, as the start-up process of a new venture may be more time-consuming for disabled people. Another example is compulsory savings or fees that are sometimes as high as 20 per cent of the loan amount. A major challenge in microcredit methodology is also the dependence on credit history. The main challenge is therefore to get the first loan so that a relationship with the microfinance institution can be established. To evaluate a possible client, a microfinance institution will assess personal skills and character in addition to the merits of the business. However, for many credit officers facing disabled people, it can be difficult to measure personal skills and character, and estimate the person's real resource base (mainly because of misunderstandings and misconceptions).

A key way to reduce exclusion is to ensure that the microfinance premises is in an accessible location; for example, that there are ramps and low counters for people in wheelchairs, or that group meetings take place in accessible venues. Accessibility also refers to access to information and communication, and so it is equally important to ensure, for example, that all the outreach campaigns or communication materials are accessible for people with visual, hearing, or intellectual impairments.

Non-financial support services for disabled people to limit self-exclusion

It is important to increase the self-confidence of disabled people and discuss with them their rights to access mainstream services, since many disabled people are wary of getting in touch with microfinance institutions. Building social skills is just as important as building business or vocational skills. Explaining to disabled people the principles of microfinance, the general requirements for applying for services, and the benefits of formal microfinance institutions (in particular, explain that microfinance is a service that has a cost; and paying that cost will guarantee access to sustainable and varied financial services) is of high importance. This may be achieved through individual coaching or through workshops and seminars. Some disabled people will require support to fill in their applications for financial services and to create their business plans – this will reduce the possibility of rejection and will identify any possible shortfalls prior to a possible failure. Building 'peer support' – inviting those who have been successful to talk and share their experiences with potential entrepreneurs is also very important for building self-confidence.

Provision of financial services by organizations of/for disabled people themselves

Most organizations *of* disabled people recognize their mission as being to advocate and defend the rights of their members. Some also provide services when these are lacking in a specific community. In contrast, organizations *for* disabled people are usually branches of international NGOs or government agencies, whose primary task is to provide services for disabled people. These activities may cover areas such as physical rehabilitation, provision of assistive devices, occupational therapy for specific groups (with intellectual, physical, or sensory impairments), education, economic inclusion programmes, and support for capacity building of local organizations of disabled people.

From our interviews, it is clear that where organizations both *of* and *for* the disabled do provide microfinance programmes, these are often relatively small, ranging from 30 to 800 borrowers. However, 14 per cent (eight organizations) reported over 1,500 members and 3.5 per cent (two organizations) reported over 10,000 members. By contrast, the specialized microfinance providers interviewed generally reach a much wider population, some with over 30,000 members.

The majority of the programmes managed by organizations of/for disabled people implemented their own income generation/microcredit programmes. Only 20 per cent of these programmes established a partnership with a specialized microfinance provider for the implementation of a microcredit scheme.

Several disabled people interviewed for this study said that their goal was to achieve inclusion in mainstream microfinance institutions instead of demanding 'special conditions' or creating alternative structures exclusive to disabled people. Such special arrangements might reinforce the idea that disabled people cannot manage a business in the same way as their non-disabled entrepreneur colleagues.

In contrast, 83 per cent of the organizations of disabled people who answered the survey stated that they have created their own structures to provide funding mechanisms, targeting exclusively disabled people. Most of them believed it would remain difficult for disabled people to join formal microfinance institutions, even in the long term. The main reasons cited for adjusting loan conditions were that: most microfinance institutions required borrowers to have an economic activity prior to receiving a loan, whereas many disabled people require the loan for start-up; and microfinance institution loan conditions did not suit the requirements of vulnerable disabled people. It was also mentioned that programmes specifically for disabled people were required because of the prejudice and stigma that prevent them from receiving loans through existing programmes, even when they comply with microfinance provider requirements.

However quite a few programmes that tried to provide financial services themselves have failed because of lack of expertise. Many of them are not self-sustainable and offer only loans and savings of low amounts. However, some have been very successful, in terms of breadth and depth of outreach, providing services to a vast number of disabled people, and reaching some of the poorest among them, for instance over 700 people in the case of Asociación de Discapacitados de la Resistencia Nicaragüense, Nicaragua, and over 4,600 in the case of the International Committee of the Red Cross in Afghanistan. But in all cases, supporting organizations remain dependent upon donor contributions because programme characteristics do not allow them to achieve operational and financial sustainability.

Conclusion

Disabled people around the world do require access to financial services to facilitate self-employment, and many have the capacity to repay loans. While it is not the case for all disabled people, some do have adequate requirements to start or expand a micro or small business through loans. Microfinance is not the only or best solution for all, but it is a powerful tool for some of the poorest and most vulnerable self-employed people.

Access for disabled people to mainstream microfinance institutions remains sporadic. Inclusion in mainstream microfinance institutions should remain the main strategy and a goal for organizations of/for disabled people. The research notes that disabled people, especially the most vulnerable, are equally likely to be 'credit-worthy' clients.

Organizations of/for disabled people are best placed to provide disabled people with support or complementary services, such as non-financial services, social work, or building self-esteem. However, many organizations of/for disabled people manage their own grant or credit programmes. Some of these have been successful in terms of the breadth and depth of outreach to disabled people, but many of them are not self-sustainable. Self-help groups may be a promising approach: they are low-cost, they respond to the needs of their members, and promote self-organization and empowerment. Self-help groups also require savings, another livelihood strategy that reduces vulnerability, and the self-help group linkage to microfinance institutions and banks makes this approach even more effective.

The study demonstrates that organizations that focus on their area of expertise perform better and provide better quality services. Complementary partnerships between microfinance institutions and organizations of/for disabled people can be set up so that each organization focuses on providing its core services to disabled people: microfinance institutions provide financial services (including loan disbursement, reimbursement, and monitoring) while organizations for disabled people provide social work.

Not all disabled people want to start a business, but those who do should have the same access to capital as any other entrepreneur. Thus, inclusion in mainstream microfinance should remain the main strategy. This research shows that simple adaptation by microfinance institutions can achieve this effectively. Two main good practices should be highlighted: information exchange between the disability sector and the microfinance sector; and changing/adapting practices to create a more inclusive society. Once microfinance and disability actors understand and trust each other, they will be more open to working together to facilitate access to truly inclusive, affordable, and sustainable financial services.

Looking at the lessons learned from this study, the goal of creating a more inclusive society will not only benefit disabled people, but other vulnerable and marginalized populations. It is clear that the Millennium Development Goals (and especially MDG1) will not be achieved without addressing the rights and needs of disabled people, who are amongst the poorest of the world's poor.

The United Nations Convention on the Rights of Persons with Disabilities (CRPD), adopted in 2006, is a powerful tool to urge all development actors to address the rights of disabled people. Article 27 of the CRPD relates specifically to the right to decent work and to earn a living. However, there remains a large gap between the international standards of the CRPD and the reality on the ground in most developing countries.

The research team hopes that this study contributes towards a broader awareness about financial inclusion; about the need to reduce the barriers faced by disabled people in accessing financial services; and about the need for disabled people to become agents of their own development.

About the author

Anne Leymat (aleymat@handicap-international.org) is the Technical Livelihoods Advisor for Handicap International. Handicap International, co-laureate of the Nobel Peace Prize, is an international organization specialized in disability and development.

Note

The full report, 'Good Practices for the Economic Inclusion of Disabled people in Developing Countries: Funding Mechanisms for Self-Employment' is available online at: http://www.makingitwork-crpd.org/miw-projects/international-level-projects/completed-projects-and-publications/. This publication is divided into two sections: the first offers an overview of the context and the second presents a guideline on providing funding mechanisms.

References

DFID (2000) *Disability, Poverty and Development*, Department for International Development, London.

World Health Organisation and World Bank (2011) *World Report on Disability*, WHO, Geneva/World Bank, Washington, DC.

Bibliography

Burjorjee, D.M., Deshpande, R. and Weidemann, C.J. (2002) *Supporting Women's Livelihoods: Microfinance that Works for the Majority – A Guide to Best Practices*, United Nations Capital Development Fund, New York.

Commission Européenne (2000) *Microfinance: Orientations Méthodologiques*, Commission Européenne, <http://www.lamicrofinance.org/content/article/detail/14581> [last accessed 2 February 2012].

Dyer, S. (2003) 'The inclusion of disabled people in mainstream micro finance programmes', paper presented at the *Staying Poor: Chronic Poverty and Development Policy Conference*, Manchester, 7–9 April 2003 [website], Leonard

Cheshire International, London <http://www.chronicpoverty.org/uploads/publication_files/CP_2003_Dyer.pdf> [last accessed 2 February 2012].

Eugene O.R. Mobility International USA (1998) *Loud, Proud and Prosperous! Report on the MIUSA International Symposium on Microcredit for Women with Disabilities*, 29 August to 8 September 1998.

Handicap International (2004) *Lessons Learned Workshop: A Review of Assistance Programs for War Wounded and other Persons with Disabilities Living in Mine-Affected Countries*, Handicap International, Paris, 25–28 May 2004.

Hashemi, S. and Rosenberg, R. (2006) *Graduating the Poorest into Microfinance: Linking Safety Nets and Financial Services* [website], Consultative Group to Assist the Poor, Washington, DC <www.cgap.org/p/site/c/template.rc/1.9.2586/> [last accessed 2 February 2012].

Hulme, D. (1995) 'Finance for the poor, poorer or poorest? Financial innovation, poverty and vulnerability', paper prepared for *Finance Against Poverty Conference*, University of Reading, 27–28 March 1995.

Ledgerwood, J. (1999) *The Microfinance Handbook: An Institutional and Financial Perspective* (Sustainable banking with the poor), World Bank, Washington, DC.

Lewis, C. (2004) 'Microfinance from the Point of View of Women with Disabilities: Lessons from Zambia and Zimbabwe', *Gender and Development* 12: May 2004.

Mersland, R. (2005) *Microcredit for Self-employed Disabled Persons in Developing Countries* [website], a study commissioned by Atlas Alliance, Oslo <http://www.microfinancegateway.org/p/site/m//template.rc/1.9.24229>[last accessed 2 February 2012].

Neufeldt, A. and Albright, A. (1998) *Disability and Self-directed Employment: Business Development Models*, IDRC, Ontario, Canada.

Standing Tall Australia and Mine Action Canada (2005) *101 Great Ideas for the Socio-Economic Reintegration of Mine Survivors*, Standing Tall Australia, Toowong and Mine Action Canada, Ottawa.

Thomas, M. (2002) 'Feasibility of integrating disabled people in savings and credit programmes in Bangladesh', *Asia Pacific Disability Rehabilitation Journal*11<www.dinf.ne.jp/doc/english/asia/resource/apdrj/z13jo0500/z13jo0509.html> [last accessed 2 February 2012].

UNCDF (2006) *Building Inclusive Financial Sectors for Development* [website], United Nations Capital Development Fund, New York < http://www.uncdf.org/english/microfinance/uploads/thematic/Building_Inclusive_Financial_Sectors_The_Blue_Book.pdf> [last accessed 2 February 2012].

Websites

The Consultative Group to Assist the Poor <www.cgap.org> an important resource with documents and focus notes on various microfinance issues.

The Microfinance Gateway <www.microfinancegateway.org>.

The MIX Market <www.mixmarket.org> information on a number of important microfinance providers around the world.

CHAPTER 5

Barriers to microcredit for disabled persons: evidence from economically active persons in Uganda

Leif Atle Beisland and Roy Mersland

Abstract

Prior research has identified five barriers hindering disabled persons' access to microcredit: exclusion by staff; exclusion by non-disabled members of credit groups; self-exclusion; exclusion by credit design; and exclusion by the disability itself. This study applies survey data to examine which barriers disabled persons themselves consider to be the most important in Uganda. The survey covers disabled persons with some kind of existing economic activity and is thus not representative of all disabled persons in the country. The data show that exclusion by credit design is the most relevant obstacle from the perspective of the disabled person. The study suggests that microfinance institutions (MFIs) should revise their credit products and make them more disability-friendly to reach out to more disabled customers. These disability-friendly products may also help the MFI to reach other poor and discriminated groups.

Keywords: microfinance, disability, Uganda, microcredit, barriers, hindering mechanisms

Persons with disabilities are a low priority and an ill-treated target group with regard to socio-economic integration (ILO, 2002; Lewis, 2004), and employers often resist hiring persons with disabilities. In developing countries, 80–90 per cent of disabled persons do not have a formal job, and most turn to self-employment (United Nations, 2007). One of the obstacles facing the self-employed is access to capital. Therefore, it is argued that access to microcredit should be a priority in pro-disability policies (Handicap-International, 2006; Cramm and Finkenflugel, 2008). The authors are fully aware of the ongoing debate on whether poor women and men benefit from accessing small loans. Based on our experience, for the purpose of this chapter, we assume that accessing microcredit, on average, is positive for poor persons with disabilities.

Bwire et al. (2009) report that only around 0.5 per cent of microfinance institution (MFI) customers are disabled. Similarly, Cramm and Finkenflugel (2008) and Martinelli and Mersland (2010) claim that few persons with disabilities have access to microfinance. This fact is not aligned with the recent

http://dx.doi.org/10.3362/9781780448879.005

United Nation Convention of the Rights of Persons with Disabilities (United Nations, 2008) which clearly indicates that persons with disabilities have the right to equal opportunities. Moreover, several authors argue that accessing credit can be of particular value to women and men with disabilities. Not only can access to capital help them build their assets and increase their businesses, but it can also increase their self-esteem and enhance their social acceptance in society (Lewis, 2004).

Simanowitz (2001) and Bwire et al. (2009) explain that several barriers exclude disabled persons from accessing microcredit: exclusion by staff because of biased attitudes; non-disabled members in credit groups; the disabled themselves because of low self-esteem and repeated experiences of rejection during life; credit design; and mobility or communication problems resulting from the disability itself. Thus far, the barrier debate has been based on anecdotal evidence and expert observations (Handicap-International, 2006; Cramm and Finkenflugel, 2008; Bwire et al., 2009; Martinelli and Mersland, 2010). This study moves the debate forwards by bringing in results from a Ugandan survey where economically active disabled persons themselves have been asked their opinions regarding the five access barriers listed above. Therefore, the barriers are analysed based on the experience and perception of the disabled persons, providing evidence of a situation, although the views may not accord completely with the reality on the ground. These issues are discussed in more detail below.

A survey carried out by the National Union of Disabled Persons in Uganda (NUDIPU) provides the data used for this study. The survey covers 841 respondents that have participated in livelihood and microfinance trainings conducted by NUDIPU. Only those disabled persons that had at least a minimum type of existing economic activity were invited to the training. Thus, the data are only representative of disabled persons involved in some kind of economic activity. Previous research on disabled persons' use of microfinance services is extremely scarce, partly because it is very difficult to get representative samples of the disabled population. Thus, even if some of our findings may not be representative of every sub-group of the disabled population, all empirical evidence on microfinance and disability should add to the limited knowledge that exists on this important topic.

One of the most important goals of the study is to provide some initial empirical evidence on the barriers that have so far been discussed mainly theoretically. Through the survey, we find that the relative importance of the five hindering mechanisms, according to the life experience of disabled persons, varies substantially. The survey shows that self-exclusion appears to be a more minor barrier than was previously assumed. Only 12 per cent of the respondents state that they would feel shy and embarrassed if they were to apply for a loan in a financial institution. In addition, exclusion by the staff and other members in the credit groups represent more relevant hindering mechanisms with 22 per cent and 30 per cent of the responses, respectively, which suggests that these barriers are important. Further, 28 per cent state that the disability itself hinders them from accessing microcredit. However, our data suggest that the main explanation for the lack of access to microcredit is dissatisfactory loan conditions and credit design. Nearly half of the respondents believe that loan conditions do not meet their needs.

The remainder of this chapter proceeds as follows: the next section reviews results from prior research, followed by a presentation of the data and the methodologies applied in our study. We then outline and discuss the results, while the final section offers a summary and conclusion to this study.

Microfinance and disability

One of the challenges faced by this study is the variability in definitions of disability. Depending on the definition applied, researchers have found that from approximately 3 per cent to nearly 20 per cent of a given population have disabilities. For example, the recent World Report on Disability by the WHO and the World Bank (2011) states that about 15 per cent of the world's population live with some form of disability. A large proportion of the persons with disabilities live in developing countries, and, in general, disability is a major explanation for extreme poverty in these places. For instance, of those who live on less than $1 a day, 1 in 5, or 20 per cent, has a disability (United Nations, 2007).

The estimated number of disabled persons in Uganda is dependent on the specific definition of disability applied, but the proportion is in any case considerable. The Population and Housing Census (2002) reported that 3.5 per cent of the Ugandan population were disabled, and the Uganda National Household Survey (2005) reported a disability rate of 7.1 per cent, whereas the Uganda Demographic and Health Survey (2006) reported 20 per cent. The distributions between types of impairment in the two former surveys are outlined in Table 5.1. Unfortunately, we are aware of no study investigating how large a proportion of the disabled population can be categorized as economically active or as potential customers of MFIs.

Regardless of the calculation method, the market for microfinance services for persons with disabilities is potentially large. This fact is in stark contrast

Table 5.1 Types of disability in Uganda

Disability type	UNHS (%)	PHC (%)	Average UNHS/PHC (%)
Vision problems	35	22	28.5
Mobility problems	25	34	29.5
Hearing problems	20	15	17.5
Other	20	29	24.5
Total	100	100	100

Source: Uganda National Household Survey (UNHS), 2005; Population and Housing Census (PHC), 2002.

to the finding by Bwire et al. (2009) that only around 0.5 per cent of MFI customers are disabled. Thus, the market opportunity for MFIs is substantial. However, one must also keep in mind that poor persons' financial partners do not only include MFIs. In Table 5.2, we refer to the types of microfinance service that disabled persons access according to the 2008 NUDIPU survey (additional details about the survey are explained below).

It is most important to note from Table 5.2 that disabled persons use microfinance services to a greater extent than previously believed. This is extensively discussed in a study by Beisland and Mersland (forthcoming), which also applies data from the NUDIPU survey. Even if the NUDIPU survey is not representative of the overall Ugandan disabled population, as it only includes those that are economically active, it is still impressive to find that 58 per cent have a savings account and that 71 per cent are members of a rotating savings and credit association (ROSCA). Disabled persons, at least those who are economically active, are not much different from other poor persons; they both save and participate in ROSCAs.

Note that, at the time of the survey, only 16 per cent of the respondents reported that they had a current loan with a bank, savings and credit cooperative (SACCO), or MFI. However, a total of 42 per cent report that they have had such a loan either presently or in the past. This suggests that even when financial institutions are able to include disabled customers, they seem unable to retain them. Thus, hindering barriers are not only about accessing MFIs for the first time but also about how to ensure that the needs of disabled customers are met, and that they therefore continue to use the services of the institution.

Data and methodology

The NUDIPU data was collected in 2008 in trainings organized for economically active disabled persons. The trainings were organized in urban centres across Uganda, and those participating were urban, semi-urban and close-by rural dwellers. With the help of local NUDIPU members and district officials responsible for disability rehabilitation, all disabled persons with some kind of economic self-employment activity were invited to participate

Table 5.2 Types of microfinance service accessed by disabled persons

Type of microfinance service	Percentage with access
Member of a ROSCA or similar	71
Saving regularly without reporting where and how	74
Saving account in a SACCO, MFI, bank or similar	58
Ever had a loan in a SACCO, MFI, bank or similar	42
Current loan in a SACCO, MFI, bank or similar	16

Note: ROSCA, rotating savings and credit association; SACCO, savings and credit cooperative in the training. The economic activity was often rather small; the smallest vegetable garden or the tiniest tomato business on a street corner was seen as an economic activity. Fifty-four per cent of the sample reported a monthly income of less than US$50. The sample covers only persons with a physical (in contrast to mental) disability. As a whole, the dataset represents physically disabled persons with existing economic activities; hence, the disabled persons are not randomly selected. The survey focuses on potential users of microfinance services and does not intend to present representative data for the overall disabled population in Uganda. However, as a starting point to better understand disabled persons' use of microfinance services, the results of the survey are interesting.

Originally, the intention of the survey was to obtain knowledge on how to enhance NUDIPU's activities for improving the livelihood of disabled persons. Barriers to microcredit were not the main topic of the survey, and thus, many questions were asked that are not relevant for this chapter. However, five of the questions are directly related to the potential five barriers hindering access to microcredit services:

1. Do you fear that the staff of the institution would reject you because of your disability?
2. If you wanted to take a loan from a financial institution, do you fear it would be difficult because existing credit groups would not accept you as member because of your disability?
3. If you were to take a loan from a financial institution, would you feel shy and embarrassed because of your disability?
4. If you were to borrow from a financial institution, would you fear that the loan conditions (e.g. amount, interest rate, loan period, etc.) may not suit your needs?
5. Would your disability make it troublesome for you to access the bank's buildings or to attend the regular meetings?

The questions were put to the disabled respondents to understand their perception of access to credit services. However, in analysis (as described below), we examined whether or not respondents had previously accessed or tried to access services to ensure that not only self-exclusion was at play in their responses.

We investigate barriers along the dimensions suggested by Simanowitz (2001) and Bwire et al. (2009) and have sorted the questions accordingly. To make the survey as accessible as possible for often illiterate or low-literate respondents, the questions could only be answered 'yes' or 'no' or 'don't know'. Any 'don't know' answers given are treated as missing and disregarded in the empirical analysis. We focus the analysis on the 'yes' percentage of the respondents that have answered the five listed questions. The fact that the sample includes only economically active persons suggests that the 'yes' percentages will be lower than in a representative sample of all persons with disabilities.

In addition to reporting the overall percentage of 'yes' answers, we also analyse the 'yes' percentage of several sub-groups in the dataset. First, answers are sorted by whether farming (arable and pastoral) is the primary source of income, type of disability, and level of education. Second, we analyse whether the answers are influenced by the respondents' own experiences with microfinance. We analyse both informal financial arrangements and formal institutional schemes (Martinelli and Mersland, 2010). The informal financial arrangements we investigate are savings (without asking how and where) and ROSCA membership. The formal institutional schemes examined are savings through an MFI, SACCO, or bank, and credit from a bank, SACCO, or MFI. Even if the questions of the survey typically focus on access to credit, it is reasonable to expect that general experience with various types of microfinance service may affect the respondents' perception of the barriers. Thus, we also include saving when investigating how previous experience with microfinance can influence the responses in the survey.

Table 5.3 lists the proportion of respondents in each of the sub-categories. The percentages are based on the actual number of respondents that have provided answers to the various sub-categories.

Empirical findings

The empirical findings are based on the experience and perception of the disabled persons themselves. Although this may not fully represent reality, in practice, the findings provide us with insight into the viewpoint of disabled customers or potential customers of microcredit services.

Table 5.3 Descriptive statistics on personal characteristics

Gender	Percentage	No. of respondents
Male	59	492
Female	41	340
Primary source of income		
Farming	50	412
Other	50	405
Type of disability		
Physical	76	593
Deaf	12	92
Blind	13	98
Education		
None	9	75
Primary	44	369
Above primary	47	388

Barrier 1: The staff

Martinelli and Mersland (2010) contend that because of attitudes and prejudices within society, the staff of an MFI, bank, or SACCO will often deliberately or unconsciously exclude persons with disabilities. A credit officer may not be able to see through the disability and recognize the real abilities of a person with a disability (Martinelli and Mersland, 2010). Table 5.4 presents our findings related to staff barriers that possibly hinder disabled persons' access to microcredit services. Only 22 per cent of the respondents fear that they will be rejected by the staff of the institution because of their disability. As described above, we also analyse differences between the sub-categories of our sample. However, note that we have dropped reporting differences related to gender because our analyses indicate that there are generally no differences to report (one minor exception; see section on 'Exclusion by credit design', below). However, we do find differences related to primary source of income, type of disability, and education level. Those whose primary source of income is farming fear rejection by staff more than the other respondents. We also note that the 'yes' percentage varies across disability type, as blind and deaf persons have a higher fear of staff rejection than those with a physical disability. Moreover, those with higher education levels appear to be less concerned about rejections than those with none or only primary education.

It is interesting to note that the persons who are already experienced users of microfinance services, in general, have a lower fear of rejection than those who are not using the services. This finding holds for both informal and formal microfinance schemes. Additionally, the finding is quite logical: the more exposed disabled persons are to microfinance, the less fear of exclusion they face. A relevant and important factor to notice is that membership in a ROSCA reduces the fear of exclusion. Hence, if the disabled persons are included in a ROSCA, this may enhance their confidence to approach formal sources of finance.

Barrier 2: Other group members

Most MFIs in Uganda practise group lending. Martinelli and Mersland (2010) maintain that a core element in group methodologies is that all members are jointly liable for each individual's loan, and the poorer and more vulnerable community members therefore risk being excluded from such groups by 'stronger' persons. The fear of exclusion by other credit groups is analysed in Table 5.5. More disabled persons fear exclusion by other credit group members than exclusion by the staff, which can be observed by the 'yes' percentage of 30 per cent compared with that of 22 per cent displayed in Table 5.4. Perceived risk or local stigmatization may discourage community members from including the disabled persons in their groups. In the sub-groups, the findings are very similar to those listed in Table 5.5.

Table 5.4 Barrier 1: Exclusion by staff (Mean for total sample: 22%; 731 respondents answered the question)
Do you fear that the staff of the institution would reject you because of your disability? "Yes" percentage:

Personal characteristics	Source of income		Disability				Education	
	Farming	Other	Physical	Deaf	Blind	No	Primary	Higher
	25%	19%	20%	26%	29%	21%	27%	16%

Microfinance experience	ROSCA		Saving		Formal saving		Loan MFI/bank	
	Yes	No	Yes	No	Yes	No	Have/had loan	Never had loan
	18%	28%	22%	21%	16%	27%	18%	25%

Table 5.5 Barrier 2: Exclusion by other group members (Mean for total sample: 30%; 726 respondents answered the question)
If you wanted to take a loan from a financial institution do you fear it would be difficult because existing credit groups would not accept you as member due to your disability? "Yes" percentage:

Personal characteristics	Source of income		Disability				Education	
	Farming	Other	Physical	Deaf	Blind	No	Primary	Higher
	32%	28%	29%	42%	33%	32%	35%	26%

Microfinance experience	ROSCA		Saving		Formal saving		Loan MFI/bank	
	Yes	No	Yes	No	Yes	No	Have/had loan	Never had loan
	26%	37%	29%	33%	25%	33%	25%	34%

Barrier 3: Self-exclusion

Persons with disabilities often experience repeated rejections and exclusions, and these negative experiences may produce secondary incapacities such as lack of self-esteem, which often lead to self-exclusion from public and private services such as microfinance (ILO, 2002). We report the results from our analysis of self-exclusion in Table 5.6. Only 12 per cent of the respondents state that they feel shy and embarrassed because of their disability. Farmers are slightly more embarrassed than others, whereas those with high education levels appear to be less shy and embarrassed. As for the disability type, the deaf stand out; the 'embarrassed' proportion is more than twice as high for this group as for the other disability categories. We also note that respondents not involved in microfinance services are more embarrassed than the rest.

According to a study by Handicap-International (2006), the suppliers of microfinance services (i.e. the MFIs) consider low self-esteem to be the main barrier hindering disabled persons in accessing their services. Among the five hindering mechanisms we investigate, by asking the disabled persons themselves, we actually report the exact opposite result. Although we must consider that this report focuses on the perception of disabled persons, direct self-exclusion appears to be the least important barrier. Further, it should be taken into account that the respondents participated in a seminar where the importance of establishing business activities and accessing microfinance services was on the agenda. To build up the self-esteem of the persons with disabilities was indirectly a part of the training. This might have led respondents to be overly optimistic in their answers to this question. A weakness of the NUDIPU study is that the respondents were not asked directly if they have ever been rejected by an MFI or bank. Moreover, it should be noted that the respondents with no experience of microfinance services are consistently more pessimistic and negative than the rest. This can be regarded as an indication that self-exclusion is more relevant than the findings on this particular question suggest.

Barrier 4: Exclusion by credit design

The design of credit services (and saving services although this is not explicitly discussed here) may create obstacles not only for disabled persons, but, because the credit methodology is often standardized and inflexible, persons with disabilities may be a particularly vulnerable group (Martinelli and Mersland, 2010). For example, mobility challenges may make weekly instalments an insurmountable obstacle. Table 5.7 presents the results when the respondents are asked if they fear that the loan conditions do not suit their needs; 46 per cent of the respondents answer 'yes'. Thus, it appears that credit design is the major reason why disabled persons do not approach MFIs.

There are few differences between the sub-groups constructed from personal characteristics. However, non-tabulated results show that males

Table 5.6 Barrier 3: Self-exclusion (Mean for total sample: 12%; 790 respondents answered the question)

If you were to take a loan from a financial institution, would you feel shy and embarrassed because of your disability? "Yes" percentage:

Personal characteristics	Source of income		Disability				Education	
	Farming	Other	Physical	Deaf	Blind	No	Primary	Higher
	13%	12%	11%	22%	9%	15%	15%	10%

Microfinance experience	ROSCA		Saving		Formal saving		Loan MFI/bank	
	Yes	No	Yes	No	Yes	No	Have/had loan	Never had loan
	9%	17%	11%	15%	10%	13%	10%	12%

Table 5.7 Barrier 4: Exclusion by credit design (Mean for total sample: 46%; 769 respondents answered the question)

If you were to borrow from a financial institution, would you fear that the loan conditions (e.g. amount, interest rate, loan period etc.) may not suit your needs? "Yes" percentage:

Personal characteristics	Source of income		Disability				Education	
	Farming	Other	Physical	Deaf	Blind	No	Primary	Higher
	47%	43%	44%	47%	50%	49%	46%	45%

Microfinance experience	ROSCA		Saving		Formal saving		Loan MFI/bank	
	Yes	No	Yes	No	Yes	No	Have/had loan	Never had loan
	42%	50%	45%	50%	46%	45%	39%	50%

are more negative than females (48 per cent vs. 42 per cent, respectively). Moreover, there is a pronounced difference between those who have or have had a formal loan compared with those who have not (a 'yes' proportion of 39 per cent vs. 50 per cent). Once again it is important to note that the respondents answer according to how they perceive the conditions. As is often the case in microfinance, poor persons are often misinformed about the real conditions of the loan, which, in practice, can be either worse or better than they tend to believe before trying them out in practice. Similarly, it should be noted that the loan condition in this study explicitly includes the interest rate level. Thus, it is difficult to disentangle high interest rates from, for instance, inflexible repayment rates. However, non-tabulated results from the survey show that 69 per cent of the respondents are willing to pay the same interest rate as non-disabled clients. Thus, 'pure' design issues appear to be significant; the results of Table 5.7 cannot solely be attributed to interest rates. Table 5.7 supports the claim of Bwire et al. (2009) that the MFIs should invest in better understanding disabled persons' needs when designing poverty-friendly products and services.

One caveat to bear in mind is how the results of Table 5.7 are to be interpreted; even if the respondents clearly indicate that they fear the loan conditions may not suit their need, we cannot necessarily attribute this finding to the fact that they are disabled. It may be the case that able-bodied clients would have answered similarly. Thus, in future research, it would be interesting to compare the findings from a survey among disabled respondents, with a control sample of non-disabled respondents. Moreover, it would be useful to identify which specific components of the loan conditions the disabled consider to be problematic.

Barrier 5: Exclusion by the disability itself

People often consider accessibility to be the main reason why disabled persons do not use microfinance services. Disabled persons can be hindered from using microcredit because the impairment may make it difficult to attend regular meetings. It may also be physically troublesome to access the banks' or MFIs' premises. Similarly, those with hearing and visual impairments face high communication barriers. For example, no MFI that we know of has information available in Braille or facilities for sign interpreters. Table 5.8 investigates this issue and shows that 28 per cent of the respondents say that the disability itself causes problems. Although the results do not support the popular claim that the disability itself is the most important hindering mechanism, the finding does suggest that physical or informational barriers are highly relevant. The disabled are not a homogeneous group and, for some, such barriers may seem insurmountable. Note that this is the only barrier where farmers are more positive than others. This may simply be due to the nature of the work itself, as farming typically requires a minimum level of physical abilities that not all disabled persons possess. We also note that respondents who are not in a

Table 5.8 Barrier 5: Exclusion by the disability itself (Mean for total sample: 28%; 782 respondents answered the question)
Would your disability make it troublesome for you to access the bank's buildings or to attend the regular meetings? "Yes" percentage:

Personal characteristics	Source of income		Disability				Education	
	Farming	Other	Physical	Deaf	Blind	No	Primary	Higher
	25%	30%	27%	33%	29%	29%	29%	27%

Microfinance experience	ROSCA		Saving		Formal saving		Loan MFI/bank	
	Yes	No	Yes	No	Yes	No	Have/had loan	Never had loan
	23%	39%	25%	34%	27%	27%	27%	28%

ROSCA seem to have the most serious problems. The finding is logical in the sense that participation in a ROSCA requires abilities to overcome mobility and communication problems.

Concluding remarks

This study uses information provided by disabled persons themselves to investigate barriers that possibly hinder them in accessing microcredit. We stress that our results are not necessarily representative of the disability community as a whole as only people with some kind of economic activity are included in the sample. Also, the findings are based on the experience and perception of disabled persons and may not fully reflect the reality on the ground. However, collectively, the findings add important knowledge to the extremely scarce literature that exists on microfinance and disability.

Our results suggest that there is some fear of rejection from the staff of the institution and from non-disabled credit-group members. Moreover, the disability itself is a major obstacle for many disabled persons. Self-exclusion, the idea that, because of low self-esteem, disabled persons do not dare approach MFIs, appears to be the least important hindering mechanism. The most important hindering barrier from the viewpoint of respondents to the survey is credit product design. Half of the respondents indicate that they fear that the credit design is not appropriate. They simply avoid taking up loans because the loan conditions do not seem to fit their needs. However, it should be noted that the design barrier could also be relevant for non-disabled persons. Moreover, loan conditions include interest rate as well as 'pure' design factors, such as loan amount and loan period, and the survey does not specifically disentangle interest rates from the other issues. Still, as more than two-thirds of the respondents state that they are willing to pay the same interest rate level as other clients, we can disregard the possibility that our findings are related to interest rates alone.

Collectively, the survey illustrates the importance of listening to the disabled persons when searching for strategies to improve their livelihoods, which in this case is to increase their access to microcredit. Our results suggest that exclusion by credit design is a significantly more important hindering mechanism than previously assumed. The policy implication is obvious: the most urgent action required to increase the access to microcredit for disabled persons is to design products to better fit the disabled persons' specific needs. Further, raising the awareness of the potential disabled customer may also increase knowledge of and access to services, as illustrated by the confidence of experienced customers. An immediate recommendation stemming from this study is that those advocating for disabled persons' rights and those offering microfinance services need to unite to better understand one another and design services appropriate to serve the needs of the disabled, and communicate this to disabled persons. However, this does not mean that MFIs should necessarily develop special products tailored for disabled customers only or that disabled customers should have subsidized interest rates. Remember that the disability community is especially heterogeneous. It would be more useful to include potential disabled customers in focus groups and panels when MFIs are developing new poverty-oriented products. Possibly, if a microfinance product is considered 'disability friendly', the product would also be friendly to most of the poor customer segments. In this regard, targeted efforts to satisfy disabled persons can be a win–win strategy for MFIs, as this may also help MFIs to better serve other poor and discriminated groups. In addition, MFIs could possibly gain from targeted marketing efforts towards the disability community.

About the authors

Roy Mersland and **Leif Atle Beisland** are from the University of Agder in Norway. Roy Mersland (roy.mersland@uia.no) has worked as a consultant for NUDIPU, the organization providing the data presented in this paper, as well as for other disability organizations. The Norwegian Association of the Disabled has sponsored this research.

References

Beisland, L.A. and Mersland, R. (2012) 'The use of microfinance services among economically active disabled persons: Evidence from Uganda', *Journal of International Development* [website], Volume 24, Issue Supplement, pp. 69–83, January 2012, http://dx.doi.org/10.1002/jid.1720.

Bwire, F.N., Mersland, R. and Mukasa, G. (2009) 'Access to mainstream microfinance services for persons with disabilities: Lessons learned from Uganda', *Disability Studies Quarterly* 29, Issue 1 <http://dsq-sds.org/article/view/168/168> [last accessed 31 January 2012].

Cramm, J.M. and Finkenflugel, H. (2008) 'Exclusion of disabled persons from microcredit in Africa and Asia: A literature study', *Asia Pacific Disability Rehabilitation Journal* 19: 15–33.

Handicap-International (2006) *Good Practices for the Economic Inclusion of Persons with Disabilities in Developing Countries*, Handicap International, Paris.

ILO (2002) *Disability and Poverty Reduction Strategies: How to Ensure that Access of Persons with Disabilities to Decent and Productive Work is Part of the PRSP Process*, International Labour Organization, Geneve, Switzerland.

Lewis, C. (2004) 'Microfinance from the point of view of women with disabilities: Lessons from Zambia and Zimbabwe', *Gender and Development* 12: 28–39, http://dx.doi.org/10.1080/13552070410001726496.

Martinelli, E. and Mersland, R. (2010) 'Microfinance for persons with disabilities', in T. Barron and J.M. Ncube (eds), *Poverty and Disability*, Leonard Cheshire Disability, London.

Simanowitz, A. (2001) 'Thematic report No. 4: Microfinance for the poorest: A review of issues and ideas for contribution of Imp-Act', in *Improving the Impact of Microfinance on Poverty*, Imp-Act, Institute of Development Studies, Sussex, UK.

United Nations (2007) 'Mainstreaming disability in the development agenda', in *Commission for Social Development*, United Nations, New York.

United Nations (2008) *Convention on the Rights of Persons with Disabilities*, United Nations, New York.

WHO/World Bank (2011) *World Report on Disability*, WHO Press, Geneva, Switzerland.

CHAPTER 6

Value chain development for rural poverty reduction: a reality check and a warning

Dietmar Stoian, Jason Donovan, John Fisk and Michelle F. Muldoon

Abstract

Over the past decade, the value chain development approach has increasingly been adopted by governments, donors, and NGOs to reduce rural poverty. The design of related interventions often assumes that poor households: 1) have sufficient resources to effectively participate in value chain development; 2) do not face substantial trade-offs when using these resources; and 3) are able to assume higher risks when reinvesting capital and labour. However, insights from our own experiences and the literature show that these assumptions often do not reflect the realities and the needs of the poor. We argue that value chain development with poor and vulnerable populations, particularly in rural areas, requires additional conceptual frameworks, analysis, and interventions. In particular, we encourage donor agencies and development practitioners to adopt an asset-based approach to the design, implementation, and assessment of target value chains and to identify the non-market interventions needed for enabling particularly disenfranchised groups to meet the minimum asset thresholds for their successful participation in value chain initiatives.

Keywords: value chain development, very poor, poverty reduction, asset-based approach, vulnerable populations

In the late 1990s, a sense of urgency over the need to reinvigorate development processes led to the formulation of the Millennium Development Goals which incorporated the view that increased income is a pre-requisite to livelihood security and a decent standard of living. To date, however, notable progress in poverty reduction – measured in terms of income and passing the $1 a day absolute poverty threshold – has mainly been made in Southeast and East Asia, especially China, while significant poverty pockets continue to persist in the rural areas of sub-Saharan Africa, South Asia, and Central and South America (UN, 2011). In search of viable alternatives to reducing poverty, value chain development emerged in the early 2000s as: 1) a market-based approach to meet poverty-related Millennium Development Goals; and 2) a response to new opportunities in international markets signalling stronger demand for

http://dx.doi.org/10.3362/9781780448879.006

agricultural and forest products and services produced with environmental and social responsibility.

Value chain development has generally been defined as an 'effort to strengthen mutually beneficial linkages among firms so that they work together to take advantage of market opportunities, that is, to create and build trust among value chain participants' (Webber and Labaste, 2010). Key concepts related to value chain development are: win–win relationships, upgrading, innovation, and added value. 'Pro-poor' value chain development has been defined as a 'positive or desirable change in a value chain to extend or improve productive operations and generate social benefits: poverty reduction, income and employment generation, economic growth, environmental performance, gender equity and other development goals' (UNIDO, 2011). It is principally from the latter perspective that many development agencies, donors, and governments have adopted value chain development as a key element of their rural poverty reduction strategies (see DFID and SDC, 2008; Humphrey and Navas-Alemán, 2010). In addition to targeting poor and vulnerable populations in the rural sector as primary beneficiaries, some value chain initiatives seek to link to the macroeconomic environment by broadening their approach towards resource-constrained enterprises in the upstream segments of a value chain, and the promotion of changes in the political-legal, institutional, and regulatory frameworks (see Kula et al., 2006).

Despite the prominent role of the value chain development approach in current development agendas, surprisingly little is known about its impacts on rural poverty. The urgency of making tangible progress towards the poverty-related Millennium Development Goals and the uncertainty about the actual and potential contributions from value chain development call for taking stock in terms of what we already know about its design, implementation, and impact, and what we have yet to learn to better direct growing investments in such initiatives and ensure substantial effects on poverty. In this chapter, we call for an asset-based approach to design, implementation, and assessment of value chain development and the need for non-market interventions to help particularly disenfranchised groups to meet the minimum asset thresholds for their successful participation in value chain development.

What we know

1. Actors promoting value chain development vary widely, as do their motives. NGOs often pursue explicit poverty reduction goals, while the private sector may see them as a by-product.

The strengthening of mutually beneficial business relationships between two or more chain actors, including producers, distributors, processors, wholesalers, and/or retailers, requires improved interactions between them, often facilitated by the provision of technical, business, and financial services from outside of the chain. Related interventions aim at strengthening capacities and enhancing mechanisms for sharing information, benefits, and risks. The stronger the win–win nature of such relations, the more likely they are to endure over time. While pro-poor value chain initiatives have an explicit focus on poverty reduction, other value chain initiatives may not. This, however, does not mean that they could not have an important, though unintended, poverty impact. Further, in many cases, a diverse set of stakeholders from within and outside of the value chain invest in the chain, at times with little or no coordination between them. Private companies, for example, may invest in their relationships with poor producers in an effort to improve their environmental and social credentials, while an NGO may provide technical and financial assistance to the producers and other chain actors. From the company's perspective, value chain development is one among several types of business strategy pursued to ensure a positive image, market positioning, and the sourcing of scarce raw materials (Box 6.1).

From the NGO's perspective, their work with upstream chain actors is in explicit pursuit of poverty reduction goals.

2. Value chain development involving the poor needs to account for their diversified livelihood strategies and related risks and trade-offs.

A review of value chain methodologies and case studies (see, for example, Kula et al., 2006; Tanburn and Sen, 2011) shows that the poverty reduction potential of value chain development is often based on the assumption that poor households: 1) have sufficient resources to effectively participate in value chain development; 2) do not face substantial trade-offs when using these resources; and 3) are able to assume higher risks when reinvesting capital and labour. In reality, however, many poor households pursue diversified livelihood strategies by combining subsistence and market-oriented agriculture with off-farm labour and other non-agricultural income-generating activities. In contrast, participation in value chain development often requires them to pursue a specialization strategy, with higher investments of capital, labour, and other resources in a given chain. Involving the rural poor in value chain

---

Box 6.1 Private sector initiatives that link to the poor

An alternative approach is the base-of-the-pyramid (BoP), where large companies aim to involve the poor in markets as providers of raw materials and/or as customers of affordable products. Such approaches often aim at producing more with less and ensuring long-term business viability. Concerns have been raised that BoP approaches underappreciate heterogeneity among the poor, as well as the intricacies of participatory partnerships between transnational companies and poor communities (Arora and Romijn, 2009). Other approaches go beyond economic goals by incorporating environmental and social goals. Corporate social responsibility (CSR) strategies call for exceeding legal mandates by involving ethical standards, stakeholder claims, and international norms in the business model. Pioneers of CSR have made notable investments in determining and improving their carbon, poverty, and other environmental or social footprints in pursuit of company or industry-wide goals. Lately, though, CSR has been criticized by Porter and Kramer (2011) for not being a solution, as social issues remain at the periphery, not at the core. Instead, they advocate creating shared value (CSV) as a strategy to generate value for both companies and society by reconceiving products and markets, redefining productivity in the value chain, and enabling local cluster development.

development therefore calls for a sound approach to address the complex trade-offs between income generation, food security, gender equity, sustainable natural resource management, and overall livelihood resilience.

According to empirical evidence, threats for the rural poor are much greater and opportunities more limited where the competitiveness of the domestic business sector lags far behind international standards (Altenburg, 2007). Under these conditions a 'multi-chain approach' to value chain development as suggested by Stoian and Donovan (2007) for agricultural and forest sectors helps to minimize risks and to maximize poverty reduction potential by strengthening not only the most promising, often export-oriented value chain, but also a variety of domestic or regional chains to which smallholders have access. Charette (2011) argues on a similar line when advocating a 'portfolio approach' to value chain development programmes that stretches across sectors, in particular where the agricultural sector is highly subject to price and weather shocks, and where the manufacturing and/or services sectors show strong potential for growth and development. Despite these recent conceptual advances in value chain development, it is still common practice to focus on a single value chain without due attention to the impact of value chain participation of the rural poor on overall livelihood resilience and related trade-offs. In any case, value chain development is only part of the solution to rural poverty reduction. A complementary focus on rural infrastructure and services, food security, and local markets for traditional products, such as basic grains, is necessary as part of a comprehensive strategy for rural development.

3. Pro-poor value chain development has both advocates and sceptics. Both sides lack sound evidence to substantiate their claims.

It does not come as a surprise that this approach has both advocates and scep-tics. The former argue that the most promising option for lifting rural people out of poverty, other than rural–urban migration, is linking poor farming house-holds to lucrative markets through skills development and new institutional arrangements along the chain. Sceptics, on the other hand, regard value chain development as unsuitable for working with the very poor, given its perceived emphasis on risk-taking and entrepreneurship, and the additional challenges faced by the very poor when responding to economic incentives (Fowler and Brand, 2011). The history of stimulating export-oriented production of non-traditional agricultural products illustrates some of the challenges faced when seeking to integrate the poor into more demanding markets (although not all value chain development programmes target export markets). From the scep-tics' perspective, such an approach may be seen as an example of failed pro-poor value chain development, while advocates would hold that precisely the absence of good value chain development practice has limited the impact of non-traditional agricultural export programmes on poverty (Box 6.2).

When looking for evidence of the impact of poverty-focused programmes it becomes evident that 'despite the pressure for measuring and reporting on results, most development agencies have in effect failed to measure and

---

Box 6.2 Struggles of smallholders to participate in non-traditional agricultural exports

Beginning in the 1970s and through the 1990s, governments and donor agencies promoted non-traditional agricultural exports (NTAE) in Latin America and Africa through trade liberalization, cooperative development, export promotion, fiscal incentives, subsidized credit, technical assistance, and infrastructure development. These initiatives were often geared towards medium and large-scale agribusinesses, while smallholders participated with varying levels of intensity without being the primary beneficiaries of NTAE interventions. In some cases, the private sector has taken the lead in organizing the production of non-traditional export goods. Food processors and supermarkets in Europe and the United States have redirected part of their sourcing of raw materials to traders, processors, and producers in developing countries. There is ample evidence that the conditions for smallholder participation in NTAE were often inadequate to allow for poverty reduction, and many of them dropped out of programmes because of low productivity, high input costs, falling export prices, and limited access to farming inputs and credit. In other cases, smallholders were pushed out as a result of their limited ability to meet the quality or volume requirements of traders and processors. Over the years, consensus has emerged that NTAE development programmes generally lacked economic sustainability, and did not adequately address poverty or the environmental and social costs of export-oriented production by large agribusinesses. Value chain development today, with its focus on both supply and demand factors for the design of sustainable market linkages, responds to the lessons learned from earlier NTAE experiences. However, there is urgent need for those that fund and implement value chain initiatives to address the poverty implications of their interventions in a more integrated way.

---

report on significant results in eradicating poverty' (Tanburn and Sen, 2011). As a result, neither advocates nor sceptics can base their claims regarding the efficacy of value chain development on sound impact assessment. In fact, most methodologies used for assessing the impact of value chain development on poverty are fairly simplistic and yield partial information on its strengths and limitations as a pathway out of poverty. Assessments typically focus on the generation of employment and income, rather than broader changes in terms of critical livelihood and business assets (see Humphrey and Navas-Alemán, 2010). Resulting reports thus provide an incomplete and potentially biased picture of value chain development impact on the livelihoods of the poor and the viability of smallholder enterprises of which they may be a part. For example, a given initiative may have increased the income derived from commercializing crop production, while at the same time it has compromised household food security and induced gender inequalities in terms of labour division and decision making; or a smallholder enterprise may have increased permanent staff, though increased payroll costs undercut the prices paid to producer members.

4. Current assessments of value chain development tend to provide an incomplete picture of their impact.

The limited utility of one-dimensional assessments follows a general trend of ineffective design and implementation of monitoring and evaluation for development interventions, including those in agriculture (Haddad et al., 2010). Discussions in the grey literature on private sector development have advocated traditional logframe-based project assessment for understanding value chain development poverty implications, with emphasis on enterprise rather than household-level impacts (see Tanburn and Sen, 2011). While logframes and similar tools for 'rigorous' planning, monitoring, and evaluation may serve the reporting needs of project managers and donors, they are inappropriate for understanding complex development processes (Jones, 2011), as they assume that the implementing organization has the capacity to achieve the targeted outcomes and impacts on its own. The failure to adequately account for external factors, such as changes in the political-legal or market context, or the effects of value chain interventions by others, provides an incomplete and potentially distorted picture of value chain development impact. The reported impact is made more questionable if household-level impacts are deduced from enterprise-level outcomes rather than by measuring them.

What we think we know

This section addresses our own insights or those of others that are yet to become part of the mainstream discussion on value chain development.

1. Conceptual models underlying pro-poor value chain development tend to lack a holistic perspective.

Many value chain initiatives involving the poor are based on fairly simple conceptual models focusing on a few variables (output, employment, income, production practices, infrastructure), while minimizing or omitting other critical, albeit complex, factors (e.g. social and human capital building, vulnerability). Such initiatives often aim to achieve greater productivity and better prices for poor households, and the resulting increase in income is seen as a proxy for poverty reduction, if not overall development. On the upside, the simplified design of a value chain initiative reduces both monitoring and evaluation, and implementation costs and makes the results easy to communicate across the chain and to other stakeholders. On the downside, such an approach does not recognize the full set of assets needed by poor households to effectively participate in value chain development, nor does it address how these assets can be built over time to permanently escape from poverty and ensure livelihood resilience, or deal with the trade-offs the rural poor face when making decisions about their allocation of time and resources between a specific value chain and other livelihood activities.

2. Poor households and smallholder enterprises require minimum assets to success-fully participate in value chain development.

Despite the warning that poor households vary in their asset levels, income flows, social networks, and abilities to cope with shocks (Fowler and Brand, 2011), many value chain initiatives treat poor rural households as a uniform stakeholder group with the same response capacity. In reality, however, both external factors such as access to basic infrastructure and services, common pool resources, and social stability, and internal factors, such as asset endowments, interests, and power, ultimately determine the extent to which poor households are 'ready' to participate in specific value chains. Similarly, the 'value chain readiness' of SMEs requires adequate policies to improve overall investment conditions, attract foreign investment, and provide better business services to increase their competitiveness (Altenburg, 2007). Minimum asset thresholds for successful participation in value chain development thus apply at both household and enterprise levels, as illustrated by an example of a coffee cooperative in Nicaragua (Box 6.3). Below these thresholds, specific, non-market-based interventions are needed to create the necessary preconditions for poor households and resource-constrained enterprises to become value chain ready.

3. Value chain development stakeholders would benefit from an asset-based approach, clear impact models, and sound metrics for understanding poverty impacts and identifying options for improved pro-poor value chain development.

There is a growing consensus that conventional poverty definitions need to be broadened to account for critical livelihood assets and vulnerability (see, for example, McKay, 2009). These definitions allow for the endowments of and

---

Box 6.3 Evidence of asset thresholds for successful participation in certified coffee markets

The Nicaragua-based coffee cooperative, Soppexcca, links roughly 500 smallholder producers to international buyers of certified fair-trade and organic coffee. Following the coffee crisis – a period between 1999 and 2004 when prices fell below the cost of production for many producers in Central America – donors and NGOs invested US$2.1 m in building the capacity of Soppexcca and its members to expand their output and better meet the quality demands of international buyers. Donovan and Poole (2011) assessed the changes in tangible and non-tangible assets for both Soppexcca and a representative sample of its members between 2006 and 2009. For the cooperative, interventions enabled major expansion of infrastructure and processing machinery, increased coverage of its technical assistance, and higher ability to engage with new fair-trade coffee buyers in the United States. Related investments provided an option for generating income through expanded service provision to members, and thus were considered critical for the co-op's long-term survival. Most co-op members benefited in terms of increased income flows and greater resilience through their membership in the cooperative. Nearly a quarter of the households were able to take advantage of credit provided by Soppexcca and others to expand their landholdings, diversify their agricultural production, and/or rejuvenate their coffee plantations. However, important weaknesses and gaps in assets remained unaddressed by the interventions and by Soppexcca itself. For example, financial assets remained seriously underdeveloped during the assessment period, while long-term debt increased significantly. Extension services expanded during the period but had difficulties in responding to members' needs. One-third of the sampled households faced major barriers to intensify coffee production, access crucial inputs and services, and increase or diversify their production of basic grains. These households tended to be strongly constrained in their endowment with or access to assets, as reflected in very small landholdings, insecure land tenure, and high dependence on off-farm income for their livelihoods. They were also more likely to have older household heads or to be headed by a female. The Soppexcca case shows that greater attention needs to be paid to the asset endowments of smallholders and the related dynamics, if value chain development is to reduce rural poverty in an integrated and significant way.

changes in human, social, natural, physical, and financial capital, and their effects on livelihood resilience. When applied in value chain development, such an asset-based approach is critical to determine whether value chain readiness is reached by meeting minimum asset thresholds. It also permits us to prove the existence of positive feedback loops; that is, processes in which the building of one asset (e.g. financial capital) leads to the building of others (e.g. human or physical capital). These would be understood as indicators of broad-based and lasting impact on rural livelihoods in pursuit of well-being and resilience.

Despite advances in thinking about the nature and causes of poverty, most sceptics and advocates of value chain development rely on a limited set of indicators and data to substantiate their poverty claims. The former tend to describe the limited poverty impact of value chain development by focusing on either the limited *relative* share of benefits captured by the poor in a given chain, or the exclusion of the poorest sections of the rural population. Advocates, on the other hand, argue that the contribution of value chain development to poverty reduction needs to be measured as an *absolute* increase in income through interventions in a value chain, and that employment effects among the poor are relevant irrespective of the overall distribution of benefits. In both cases, clear impact models with plausible cause–effect relationships, or refined metrics that allow for both positive and negative effects of value chain development are largely absent.

There is an urgent need and an opportunity for public and private investors in value chain development to promote the adoption of an asset-based approach to the design and implementation of value chain initiatives, based on well-defined impact models, and to develop sound metrics that help demonstrate under which conditions value chain development generates high poverty impact. Recent work by an international coalition of development practitioners and researchers highlights the opportunities and the challenges for the application of an asset-based approach to value chain development (Box 6.4).

4. Value chain development requires adequate linking of technical, business, and financial services.

In addition to successful collaboration between public and private sectors and civil society, pro-poor value chain development requires a combination of technical, business, and financial services. Some of these services are available from within the chain, particularly those that help improve quality or efficiency. Such 'embedded services', typically provided by downstream actors to their upstream business partners, have the advantage of focusing on clearly identified needs and upgrading opportunities in the chain. On the other hand, certain services may not be readily available from within the chain, especially those that help improve environmental and social performance or that address long-term issues related to capacity building and skills development among the poor. These services may need to be sourced from external service providers, such as government agencies, NGOs, development projects, and

---

Box 6.4 International collaboration to design an asset-based approach to value chain development assessment

Between 2008 and 2011, an international group of development practitioners and researchers, representing Bioversity International, CATIE, CRS, ICRAF, Intercooperation, LWR, MEDA, Swisscontact, TechnoServe, and Winrock's Wallace Center, among others, collaborated on the design and testing of the 5CapitalsToolkit – an asset-based approach to assess the poverty impacts of value chain development (see Donovan and Stoian, 2010). In collaboration with local NGOs and consultants, and with financial support from the Ford Foundation, the toolkit was designed and validated through 23 case studies in Latin and North America, Africa, and Asia. The aim was to design a tool that would: 1) assess the impact of a whole set of value chain development interventions, rather than that of a particular intervention; 2) consider changes in assets among both households and the enterprises that maintained links with them; and 3) differentiate between the impacts of the combined value chain development interventions vis-à-vis those induced by external factors. Experiences gained in tool testing demonstrated the potential of an asset-based approach to value chain development assessment, along with related challenges. Case study collaborators agreed that: 1) such an approach is very useful to gain in-depth insight into value chain development-related poverty impacts; 2) the focus on both household and enterprise assets sheds additional light on poverty impacts; 3) the context analysis as the first step of the methodology is critical to isolate value chain development-related impact from context-induced change; and 4) the results of impact assessment have highest value when used for redesigning value chain development interventions. At the same time they found that this approach: 1) implies investments of human and financial resources that are reasonable but not low-cost; 2) requires a flexible handling of the enterprise assessment due to the varied nature of 'linked enterprises'; and 3) depends on systems thinking to make the most out of it. The final version of the toolkit (in English and Spanish) and an edited case study volume will be made available on the CATIE and ICRAF websites in 2012 (www.catie.ac.cr and www.icraf.org).

---

consulting firms. The diverse nature of the services needed poses a challenge to their effective and efficient delivery. Technical services related to production and, to a lesser extent, processing technologies tend to be readily available for traditional products, either from downstream actors or from external service providers. Financial services may be provided in the form of advance payments or credits within the chain, or through government-funded programmes and microfinance projects from outside the chain. Usually, however, they are not available to highly resource-constrained smallholders. Business services often turn out to be the Achilles heel in value chain development as specialized business service providers for the rural sector are largely absent. A further challenge for value chain development-related services is their provision in an isolated fashion. Service providers are typically specialized in one of these three types of service and rarely make an effort to partner with those who provide complementary services. Effective and efficient services for value chain development require a sound demand analysis and a concerted approach to the delivery of technical, business, and financial services that are well-linked and complement each other in a logical fashion. Following the subsidiarity principle, only those services would be provided from outside the chain that cannot be sourced from within the chain.

What we still need to know and do differently

The number of rural people living in desperate conditions under various degrees of vulnerability remains high. Undoubtedly, we have advanced our understanding of poverty issues and there is a growing consensus on the importance of pro-poor interventions in value chains. Yet there are a number of crucial issues on which our knowledge is still insufficient. In the absence of an asset-based approach to designing, implementing, and monitoring value chain initiatives, related impact models and theories of change are incomplete. Under these conditions, it is virtually impossible to identify the best options for helping poor people to *exit* from poverty, let alone to *stay* out of poverty. In addition to these knowledge gaps, there are a number of 'action gaps' related to areas that require forms of engagement in value chains in addition to, or other than, those applied to date.

Need for improved knowledge

1. *How to determine value chain readiness?* If the goal of the intervention is to reduce vulnerability and lift people out of poverty, how can we determine whether poor households and their business organizations are ready to participate in value chain development? Which minimum asset thresholds do they need to meet and, if not available, what are the best options to help them become value chain ready?

2. *Can asset building at the level of smallholder enterprises spur asset building at the household level?* Since business organization of smallholders is often considered a prerequisite for their successful participation in value chains, we need to understand under what conditions asset building at the level of the smallholder enterprises positively influences household assets and reduces vulnerability, and how value chain development can help to create more synergy in this respect.

3. *How to ensure that assessing value chain development impact is both effective and efficient?* Current impact assessment of value chain programmes tends to be low-cost and fairly one-dimensional, whereas an asset-based approach to assessment yields more robust results while requiring higher investments. There is a clear need for experimenting with differentiated approaches to impact assessment, for example the routine measuring of outputs, the assessing of outcomes to the extent possible, and full-fledged impact assessment through in-depth case studies. The Donor Committee for Enterprise Development (DCED), for example, recommends three 'universal' impact indicators (scale, income, and jobs) for ongoing results measurement; at the same time it acknowledges that this cannot replace rigorous impact assessments, nor evaluations, as these ask broader questions (Tanburn and Sen, 2011).

4. *How best to use an asset-based approach for planning, implementing, and assessing value chain development?* In particular, we need to better understand what indicators within each asset type – typically including

human, social, natural, physical, and financial capital – tell us the most about reducing poverty and vulnerability. Which proxies can be used to make assessment manageable and cost effective? How do we adapt or tailor value chain development to different contexts and varying asset levels in given populations? How can we best deal with non-linear asset pathways (asset building followed by asset erosion or vice versa)?

5. *Which roles correspond to private, public, and civil society sectors in promoting value chain development?* What can the private sector do alone? Under what conditions will the private sector invest in the long term, or go the extra mile for pro-poor value chain development? What can realistically be expected from private sector initiatives, such as base of the pyramid, corporate social responsibility, or creating shared value? Where and how do public–private partnerships work best and where are their limits? What is the specific role of NGOs in helping build assets beyond the contributions from public and private sectors?

Need for improved action

1. *Account for the evolution of income and asset objectives.* Value chain development programmes need to account for the dynamics and variations of asset endowments and livelihood objectives among poor and vulnerable populations. Different measures are needed in each stage when following a pathway out of poverty from: '(i) stabilizing household consumption/stemming asset loss, to (ii) smoothing household consumption/protecting assets, to (iii) smoothing household income/acquiring assets, to (iv) expanding household income/leverage assets, and to (v) stabilized income-generation and asset accumulation' (Fowler and Brand, 2011).

2. *Differentiate between those who are value chain ready and those who are not.* Market-based interventions work for those who meet minimum asset thresholds and, hence, are value chain ready. Those who are not require specific, non-market-based interventions to create the necessary preconditions for their participation in value chain development. These include, but are not limited to, customized technical assistance and training to build human and social capital, rehabilitation of natural capital where eroded, investments in basic infrastructure and services, and resolution of land tenure conflicts where existing. These interventions fall outside the realm of value chain development but are critical for its success, if the poorest sections of the rural population are to benefit from it.

3. *Follow logical sequence of asset building.* There are plentiful examples of programmes where donors have given processing equipment to farmer organizations, but the initiatives have failed because of lacking business skills. In many cases, human and social capital needs to be built before considering investments in physical capital. In other cases, eroded natural capital needs to be rebuilt before meaningful business development is possible.

4. *Ensure synergies among public and private sectors and civil society, promoting value chain development.* Based on the subsidiarity principle, public sector and civil society should only engage in those interventions that cannot be performed by the private sector. This requires determining which services can be provided from within the chain ('embedded services') and which need to be sourced from external service providers (in many cases government agencies or NGOs). For example, rather than donating equipment, donors might link farmers to credit agencies to buy the equipment. If necessary, agencies could subsidize the cost of credit.

5. *Improve the quality of and the linking between technical, business, and financial services.* In the absence of integrated service providers, we need to make major efforts to link technical, business, and financial services in ways that allow for meaningful asset building at household and smallholder enterprise levels. At the same time, we need to ensure that these services are geared to the requirements identified by the chain actors rather than outside agents from public sector or civil society.

6. *Create awareness among donors and development practitioners about the advantages of adopting an asset-based approach to the design, implementation, and assessment of value chain development.* There is a need to provide evidence that the increased costs and complexity of an asset-based approach are outweighed by tangible benefits in terms of higher impact on poverty reduction, livelihood resilience, and viability of smallholder enterprises.

7. *Promote comprehensive strategies to rural development.* There is both a need for and an opportunity to combine value chain development with other approaches to rural development, such as sustainable rural livelihoods, territorial development, and investments in rural infrastructure and services.

8. *Innovate in partnerships for joint learning and continuous improvement.* The diverse nature of stakeholders in value chain development provides a great opportunity for joint learning. Each of them brings specific perspectives, skills, and experiences to the table, but we need to define appropriate forums and mechanisms for sharing and capitalizing on these. The outcome of such learning alliances and communities of practice will be highest if nurtured by genuine interest in learning and authentic commitment to continuous improvement.

Conclusions

Our current knowledge of the poverty impacts of value chain development is limited. Regardless of whether related initiatives are driven by private, public, or civil society sectors, the use of sound metrics to determine their impact at both the enterprise and the household level, and to isolate value chain development from context-induced change should be the rule rather than the exception. If value chain development is to be effective in addressing rural poverty, it must embrace the complex needs and realities of the rural poor. This includes the recognition that market-oriented activities are important but not exclusive elements of rural livelihood strategies. Particular attention needs to be paid to the specific challenges and needs of the very poor given their higher risk and vulnerability. Otherwise there is a substantial risk that pro-poor value chain development does not live up to expectations and causes undue trade-offs in the livelihood strategies of the rural poor.

An asset-based approach to the design, implementation, and assessment of value chain development is a powerful vehicle to address these challenges and risks. Not only does it provide an appropriate measure of the multiple dimensions of poverty and vulnerability, but it also helps to determine which households and smallholder enterprises are ready for value chain development, and which require specific preparatory interventions to become value chain ready. An asset-based approach to value chain development comes at a price, though. Related planning, data collection, and analysis are relatively time-consuming, complex, and costly. At the same time, such an approach helps forgo higher expenses to mitigate unintended effects of interventions in value chains. It provides public sector and civil society organizations with the necessary information to justify the investment of taxpayers' money, and holds the potential to improve the environmental and social credentials of private sector companies pursuing base of the pyramid, corporate social responsibility, creating shared value, or similar strategies.

Value chain development is not a panacea to rural development. When seeking impact beyond poverty reduction on resilience of livelihoods and ecosystems, it needs to be paired with complementary approaches. Comprehensive strategies for rural development would include improvements in local infrastructure and services, political-legal frameworks, food security, local markets for agricultural and forest products, and income generation through services and off-farm employment. Appropriate design, implementation, and monitoring and evaluation of such strategies, again, will best be achieved by pursuing an asset-based approach.

Much remains to be learned about the best possible design and implementation of value chain programmes and pertinent combinations with other approaches. Undoubtedly, however, an asset-based approach to pro-poor value chain development is a critical piece of such strategies. Governments, donors, development agencies, NGOs, and private sector agents committed to poverty reduction will need to invest in pilot projects, tool development, and capacity building; engage in multi-stakeholder platforms for joint learning; and commit to continuous improvement. Without the adoption of an asset-based approach to value chain development, poor households and smallholder enterprises in the upstream segments of the chain will continue to be exposed to high uncertainty and risk and, in particular, to potentially harmful trade-offs between value chain optimization and resilience at the household and business level.

About the authors

Dietmar Stoian (stoian@catie.ac.cr) is Leader, Program of Competitiveness and Value Chains, Tropical Agricultural Research and Higher Education Center (CA TIE), Turrialba, Costa Rica; **Jason Donovan** is Marketing Specialist with the World Agroforestry Centre (ICRAF), Lima, Peru; **John Fisk** is Director and **Michelle F. Muldoon** is Program Officer of the Wallace Center at Winrock International, Arlington, VA, USA.

References

Altenburg, T. (2007) *Donor Approaches to Supporting Pro-poor Value Chains* [website], report prepared for the Donor Committee for Enterprise Development – Working Group on Linkages and Value Chains, German Development Institute (DIE), Bonn, Germany <www.value-chains.org/dyn/bds/docs/568/DonorApproachestoPro-PoorValueChains.pdf> [last accessed 24 January 2012].

Arora, S. and Romijn, H. (2009) *Innovation for the Base of the Pyramid: Critical Perspectives from Development Studies on Heterogeneity and Participation* [website], United Nations University/Maastricht Economic and Social Research and Training Centre on Innovation and Technology, Maastricht, the Netherlands <www.merit.unu.edu/publications/wppdf/2009/wp2009-036.pdf> [last accessed 24 January 2012].

Charette, D. (2011) *A Portfolio Approach to Value Chain Development Programs*, MicroREPORT #169, USAID, Washington, DC.

DFID (Department for International Development) and SDC (Swiss Development Corporation) (2008) *A Synthesis of the Making Markets Work for the Poor (M4P) Approach*, SDC, Berne, Switzerland.

Donovan, J. and Poole, N. (2011) 'Asset building in response to value chain development: Evidence from specialty smallholder coffee producers in Nicaragua', *ICRAF Working Paper* 138, World Agroforestry Centre, Nairobi, Kenya.

Donovan, J. and Stoian, D. (with contributions from Antezana, I., Belt, J., Clark, S., Harper, M., Poole, N., Ruddick, S. and Waagbo, J.) (2010) *Assessing the Impact of Value Chain Approaches on Rural Poverty*, Methodological Guidelines for Development Practitioners and Private Sector Representatives, CATIE, Turrialba, Costa Rica.

Fowler, B. and Brand, M. (2011) *Pathways Out of Poverty: Applying Key Principles of the Value Chain Approach to Reach the Very Poor*, Discussion Paper/ Microreport #173, USAID, Washington, DC.

Haddad, L., Lindstrom, J. and Pinto, Y. (2010) 'The sorry state of M&E in agriculture: Can people-centred approaches help?' *IDS Bulletin* 41: 6-25.

Humphrey, J. and Navas-Alemán, L. (2010) 'Value chains, donor interventions and poverty reduction: A review of donor practice', *IDS Research Report* 63, IDS, Brighton, UK.

Jones, H. (2011) 'Taking responsibility for complexity: When is a policy problem complex, why does it matter, and how can it be tackled?' *ODI Briefing Paper* 68, ODI, London.

Kula, O., Downing, J. and Field, M. (2006) 'Value chain programmes to integrate competitiveness, economic growth and poverty reduction', *Small Enterprise Development* 17: 23-35.

McKay, A. (2009) 'Assets and chronic poverty: Background paper', *Chronic Poverty Research Centre Working Paper* 100, University of Sussex, Brighton, UK <www.chronicpoverty.org/uploads/publication_files/WP100%20McKay_1.pdf> [last accessed 24 January 2012].

Porter, M.E. and Kramer, M.R. (2011) 'Creating shared value: How to reinvent capitalism and unleash a wave of innovation and growth', *Harvard Business Review* (Jan-Feb 2011): 2–17.

Stoian, D. and Donovan, J. (2007) 'Value chain development from a livelihoods perspective: A multi-chain approach for coffee and cacao producing households in Central America', in E. Tielkes (ed.), *Utilisation of Diversity in Land Use Systems: Sustainable and Organic Approaches to Meet Human Needs. Tropentag 2007 – International Research on Food Security, Natural Resource Management and Rural Development*, Kassel-Witzenhausen, Germany, 9–11 October 2007.

Tanburn, J. and Sen, N. (2011) *Why Have a Standard for Measuring Results? Progress and Plans of the Donor Committee for Enterprise Development*, DCED, London.

UN (United Nations) (2011) *The Millennium Development Goals Report 2011*, UN, New York.

UNIDO (United Nations Industrial Development Organization) (2011) *Pro-poor Value Chain Development: 25 Guiding Questions for Designing and Implementing Agroindustry Projects*, UNIDO, Vienna, Austria.

Webber, C.M. and Labaste, P. (2010) *Building Competitiveness in Africa's Agriculture: A Guide to Value Chain Concepts and Applications*, World Bank, Washington, DC.

CHAPTER 7

Catalysts of agricultural supply markets: the case for smart subsidies in Zambia

Alexandra Snelgrove and Lemmy Manje

Abstract

The decision to purchase new productive technologies, however promising, presents great risks for the rural poor. The result is that farmers are disinclined to purchase new technologies, and manufacturers, wholesalers and retailers are unwilling to invest in inventory and supply. To break this chain, smart subsidies can be used to accelerate demand and supply for critical production technologies. Properly administered incentives can attract commercial suppliers to actively address the needs of rural, underserved smallholder farmers without creating dependency. This article presents the case of smallholder farmers in Zambia to highlight how incentives can play a role in developing weak agribusiness service markets.

Keywords: vouchers, smart subsidy, irrigation, agricultural input suppliers, Zambia

Better farming inputs and appropriate agricultural technologies such as improved irrigation pumps and drip irrigation systems can enhance agricultural productivity for farmers regardless of size. Yet smallholder farmers with meagre incomes typically make choices that avoid the risk of unknown effective technologies – however appropriate or productive these might be. The response by some development practitioners is to introduce new farming technologies through free distribution. This often leads to limited scale and outreach with distorted, weak agricultural input supply markets. Such programmes also fail to impart a spirit of entrepreneurship among the recipients of the technologies.

This article presents an alternative approach to accelerate technology adoption – namely discount vouchers. Mennonite Economic Development Associates' (MEDA) current project in Zambia is used as a case study to highlight the role of smart subsidies in economic development. The term 'smart subsidy' should be understood as not having a market distortion effect or creating a donor dependency. Through the project, incentives have been used to address risk aversion among smallholder farmers in testing new and productive technologies. The private sector has also been engaged with the message that smallholder farmers, not just NGOs, are valued customers of agricultural inputs and technologies. This article argues that smart subsidies

http://dx.doi.org/10.3362/9781780448879.007

can develop weak agribusiness markets by enabling private sector firms to realize the value of serving the needs of small enterprises. It includes a discussion on the merits of the discount approach in addition to factors that ensure sustainability of project impacts after the discounts are withdrawn.

Background situation of Zambian farmers

In 2008, Zambia ranked 163 out of 179 countries on the United Nations Human Development Index (HDI) (United Nations Development Program, 2008). It is interesting to note that while the HDI score for Sub-Saharan Africa as a region has increased (though nominally), Zambia's HDI score has decreased over the last 20 years. Over 63.8 per cent of the population manages to survive on less than a dollar a day (UNDP, 2008). The population is also geographically dispersed with 65 per cent living in rural areas (UNDP, 2008).

The failure of agriculture in Zambia is one of the major contributors to rural poverty (Government of Zambia, 2002). The majority of the country's population (70 per cent) relies on agricultural activities for their livelihoods; as such the sector drives the country's economic growth. Increasing agricultural productivity is therefore a critical component of Government of Zambia's Poverty Reduction Strategy Paper (PRSP) with the horticultural sector playing a key role. Demand for fruit and vegetables is high given the prevalence of vegetables in the local diet plus the strong export market (regional and European) (Government of Zambia, 2006). Yet most small-scale farmers in Zambia currently produce for subsistence purposes only; in fact, only one in five smallholder farmers actually produce horticulture crops for sale (Hichaambwa and Tschirley, 2006).

Farmers living along the main highways and rail line are more likely to be connected to markets and are in a better position to exploit commercial opportunities. In order to sell to these markets, smallholder farmers must be able to address a myriad of issues such as weak market linkages, inadequate support services and high production costs. Farmers with appropriate irrigation technologies are able to transition from rain-fed cereal crops to production of high-value vegetable crops. Low-cost technologies such as treadle pumps, hip pumps and drip irrigation systems provide more efficient water use, labour-saving benefits, extended growing seasons and the ability to produce in the off-season. Studies have shown that through the adoption of these technologies farmers earn, on average, an additional $100 in net income per annum (Frausto, 2000). International Development Enterprises has found that this figure may be potentially higher in Zambia given the limited suppliers currently producing horticultural crops (Frausto, 2000).

Irrigation technology dissemination in Zambia

MEDA's assessment in Zambia focused on water resources and access to appropriate and affordable water technologies with identification of effective ways to both stimulate demand, without creating dependency, and strengthen supply, without weakening investment and entrepreneurship on the part of the suppliers.

Most readers of this journal would likely agree that free handouts of these technologies would have significant adverse consequences. Free distribution would distort the market and make it difficult for private sector actors to enter this line of business; access to technologies would therefore only last as long as the project period. Similar experiences with subsidized fertilizers in Zambia have highlighted the issues with this approach. For example, according to the World Bank, the Fertilizer Support Program (FSP), which aimed to improve food security and alleviate poverty through provision of subsidized fertilizer, suffered from high costs and administrative inefficiencies. Not only did the project crowd out private sector input dealers, there was evidence that the targeting was inaccurate and that the actual cost of the project was greater than the value of additional maize produced (Gregory, 2006).

Alternatively, MEDA could have explored supply-side strategies to enhance the technology market. Matching grant programmes for technology manufacturers and importers might have provided these firms with the incentive to improve their production processes or efficiencies. Unfortunately, matching grants often do little to replicate the market with impact beyond the life of the project (McVay and Miehlbradt, 2006). And while a matching grant may stimulate supply, it would not nurture the nascent demand for these technologies. MEDA could have also developed a training programme for suppliers to enhance their marketing capacity or developed a quality control system to address product issues. Both are important elements to building the market, however, these activities alone would not have been sufficient. Farmers would still be hesitant to try the technology and suppliers would continue to remain in Lusaka selling their technologies from the capital.

The voucher approach

MEDA decided to focus instead on demand-side interventions as a way to accelerate the market for these technologies. It was understood that enhancing adoption rates requires substantial behaviour change through scaled demonstrations of the positive benefits from appropriate technologies.

In the value chain development context, vouchers have primarily been used for subsidized training to microentrepreneurs. One of the first projects to use this approach was the Kenya Micro and Small Enterprise Training and Technology Project, financed by the World Bank. Using a demand-side subsidy, the project provided vouchers to small enterprises to encourage their participation in technical and business management courses; these discounts provided an incentive for commercial training providers to enter this market (World Bank, 2005; Hallberg, 2006). There has also been a call for the use of vouchers as a way to ensure more market-oriented relief programmes that allow target beneficiaries to purchase food and other goods from local retailers (McVay and Miehlbradt, 2006).

Other studies have highlighted the role that vouchers can play in stimulating the market for inputs, specifically fertilizers and seed (Gregory, 2006). While there have been issues with some of these programmes, input vouchers have been seen as having the potential to operate as a pro-poor, smart subsidy to help subsistence farmers transition to cash crops (Gregory, 2006). For example, a voucher programme in Nigeria for fertilizers showed that almost half of the farmers had better access to fertilizers, while dealers felt that they had better stock security (Gregory, 2006). Critics of the voucher approach may argue that the use of vouchers for small-scale producers hinders sustainability. However, these examples show that vouchers are not necessarily market distortive subsidies; they can be effective mechanisms to develop links between producers and supply chains.

The voucher strategy appealed to MEDA as an alternative to the previous handout approach because:

- Vouchers do not hide the real cost of the technology. Farmers are aware that the discount provided is in fact a price reduction (which is viewed as being offered by the suppliers).
- The voucher is offered as a clear one-time cost reduction from suppliers; this is not an ongoing price subsidy but rather a promotion to allow farmers to test the technology. Each farmer is given a period in which to redeem the voucher, after which the voucher expires. The discount voucher is designed along the lines of common commercial product promotion models that are typically undertaken by private sector to allow customers to test a new product.
- Research has shown that farmers are more likely to apply and use technologies when purchased as opposed to being provided for free. As such, they also serve to automatically direct the limited subsidy to farmers who are most likely to use the voucher efficiently.
- Farmers are still required to pay for the majority of the technology cost. As farmers are rational consumers, it can therefore be expected that only those who want to enhance their production under irrigation will take up the offer.
- Vouchers create demand that draws a commercial network into rural areas, increases the capacity of retailers to invest in inventory, and strengthens the technology market for future clients.
- By enticing suppliers to enter the market, after-sales service is now available for technology users. This was not the case when technologies were distributed for free as maintenance services and spare parts markets were not developed.

MEDA's voucher Programme

The goal of MEDA's market development programme is to accelerate supply and demand for appropriate and affordable water technology products without

Farmers get trained on irrigation technologies and practices 1	Farmers receive discount vouchers upon training completion or technology demonstration 2	Farmers use their top-up cash and vouchers to purchase technologies from the technology dealers 3
MEDA reimburses manufacturers and distributers 6	Technology manufacturers and distributers submit vouchers for reimbursement to MEDA 5	Farmers get trained on irrigation technologies and practices 4

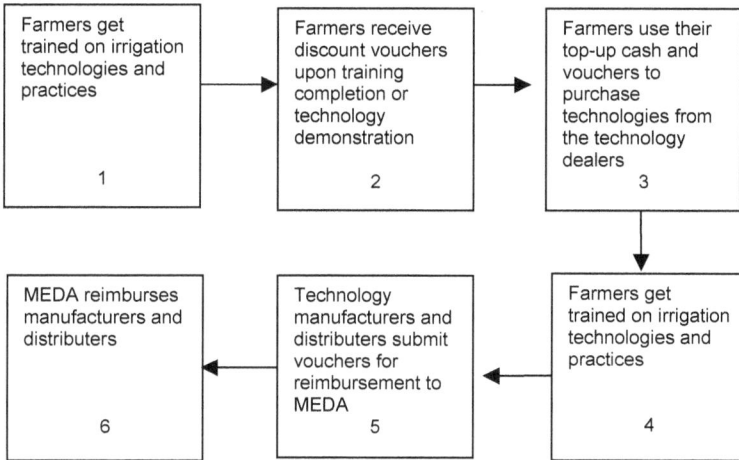

Figure 7.1 Market stimulation model

dependency while strengthening local businesses to ensure their long term viability and sustainable reach to underserved rural populations in Zambia. Originally the voucher value was set at approximately $50. A variable voucher approach (with a discount of 40 per cent) will be used by the programme in future. The discount value was set based on the market conditions and indicative willingness-to-pay, with flexibility to respond to market changes as the interactions between suppliers and farmers evolve (see Figure 7.1).

New irrigation technologies and agricultural best practices were taught and demonstrated through training sessions, agricultural fairs and other information sessions organized by MEDA's partners and the irrigation suppliers. Partners include International Development Enterprises and Zambian National Farmers Union. After attending these sessions, farmers are entitled to a discount certificate to purchase their preferred irrigation technology. However, the discount is only for a portion of the cost; farmers are required to contribute the remaining amount through their own savings or other sources of income. Recipients then take their certificate to one of a number of registered retail outlets to purchase their preferred technology. Retailers are able to submit redeemed certificates to water technology manufacturers and importers in exchange for new inventory while still maintaining their mark-up. The manufacturers and importers then redeem the certificates with MEDA. All voucher transactions are conducted electronically via an SMS (short messaging service) system.

While there have been a number of voucher programmes for small enterprise development, the commercial model adopted and facilitated by MEDA represents some new perspectives on voucher programme management in the context of market development:

- Invisibility of MEDA. Most voucher programmes do not insist on in-visibility for the funding organization. It is typical for the vouchers to carry the logos of the funding organization. In the context of market development, remaining outside the supply chains is a key determinant to a smooth exit strategy. Experience shows that once voucher recipients know the source of funds is a development organization, they are likely to request additional discounts thereby reducing prospects for a sustainable market. Under the voucher programme, MEDA strives to maintain its invisibility; the vouchers, for example, carry the logo of the suppliers not MEDA.

- Technology sales are made through the suppliers' commercial outlets and agents. While other voucher programmes would use both public and private sector for voucher distribution, management and redemptions, MEDA has insisted on a purely private sector driven model for sustainability. Therefore, the commercial sector handles the logistics of technology distribution, marketing, storing, transporting and selling the technologies. Owing to supply-side weaknesses, MEDA has provided complementary support activities but without further subsidization of service provision.
- Use of a commercially driven model allows for expansion and availability of technologies in all the places where vouchers are distributed; suppliers have been more willing to invest in retail networks in geographic locations where they know that there is effective demand.
- Rather than create parallel markets for technology distribution, the voucher programme attracts new investment from existing and new private sector suppliers, fostering competition and increasing options and technology choices for farmers.
- Use of electronic vouchers based on an SMS application serves as a real-time monitoring tool and acts as a new planning tool for investments by suppliers. The SMS application has served as the first tier for fraud control; the message to farmers has been that the voucher is 'electronically' monitored and not transferable.

These added dimensions allow MEDA to be innovative in its voucher programme and advance the thinking on voucher delivery in a technology promotion context.

In order for the project to achieve the intended goal, a number of critical design issues needed to be addressed, including the following:

- Suppliers and retailers sign on to the voucher programme to directly market water technologies and use the discount voucher as part of their sales strategies. MEDA is invisible and the discount is seen as a promotion coming directly from technology suppliers allowing farmers to test and see the benefits of the technologies.
- There is transparency on the real price to the smallholder farmers.
- Technology suppliers are encouraged to be proactive in direct marketing and sales of the technologies to smallholder farmers, including

establishment of appropriate distribution networks and technology demonstration activities.

- The discount vouchers operate as electronic vouchers, which facilitates real-time monitoring and performance tracking while addressing fraud issues.
- MEDA and its implementing partners are completely outside the water technology supply chain. Some of the agribusiness organizations MEDA works with are development organizations that are new to market development approaches and therefore MEDA continues to provide technical assistance to ensure all key stakeholder organizations understand market development best practices.

While the vouchers are an important component towards building the irrigation technology service market, it is not the only area of activity. Complementary activities, such as training of suppliers on marketing, support for farmers to access new markets, and financial services linkages will be critical to the project's success. Related activities currently implemented by the project will be downloaded to the private sector as part of the project's exit strategy once these firms understand the merit of these efforts and are willing to invest resources in continuing these initiatives. For example, MEDA organized agri-fairs where the different participating suppliers had the opportunity to demonstrate their various product offerings. Next irrigation season these sessions will be organized by the suppliers themselves. The expectation is that as suppliers see the benefit in reaching out to farmers and invest in marketing activities, further interventions by MEDA will no longer be required. MEDA has not partnered with NGOs who wish to be both market facilitators and direct technology providers and therefore is able to stay out of the supply chain. As the demand for the technologies grows, MEDA is able to concentrate on developing long-term solutions for continued access, including development of appropriate financial products for technology acquisition. The expectation is that as the vouchers are withdrawn, demand for the technologies will be raised, suppliers will understand the importance of investing in marketing and distribution, and microfinance institutions will have an appropriate product that assists farmers in the upfront capital cost of these technologies.

Figure 7.2 shows the market development framework being implemented in Zambia:

Overview of project with results

The project has recently finished its first year of operation. Initial results and anecdotal evidence have highlighted the positive potential impact through the discount approach. In the previous irrigation season, over 3,500 vouchers were distributed with close to 500 redeemed. Critics may argue that the level of redemption appears low when compared to typical voucher programmes. Important to note is that the cost of the pump still represents a large capital investment

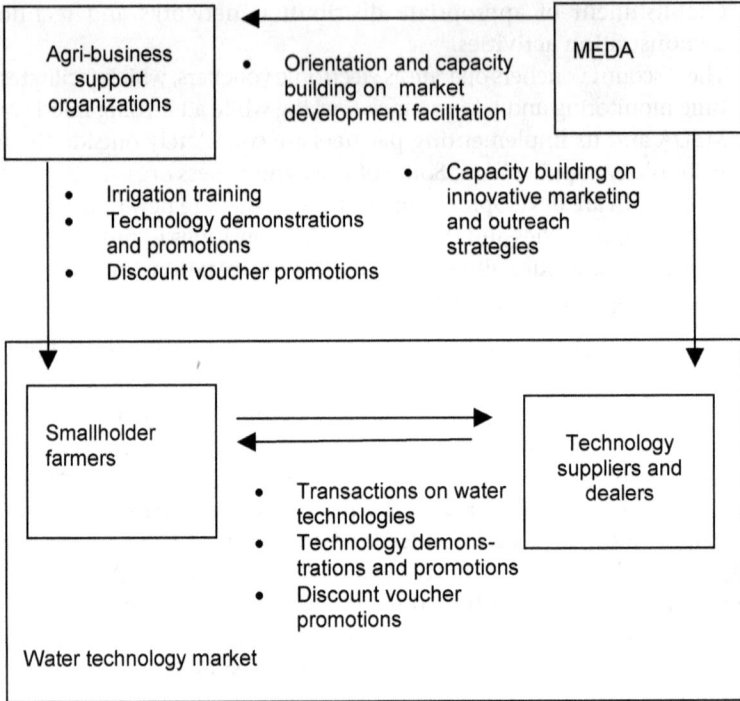

Figure 7.2 Voucher programme market development model

for farmers, particularly in comparison to the price of a training course. Due to issues with supplier inventory and distribution network management, suppliers failed to take advantage of the prime irrigation season (April to June) leaving some of the stimulated demand unserved. This meant that the expectation of higher redemption rates was not realized. In order to ensure that the project achieves desired scale, the project team has identified a range of strategies to engage suppliers more deeply in marketing and inventory investment. The voucher performance in the first irrigation season should be evaluated in the context of the degree of the market deficiencies and weaknesses that accounted for the pace at which technology suppliers have taken up the business opportunity. A year would therefore serve as a learning opportunity for suppliers to address risk aversion, reorganize their investments and map out strategies to adequately respond to the emerging market opportunities. In a market development programme, qualitative changes are good pointers of long-term sustainable market changes, expected once the market actors have fully embraced the market opportunities. This is the context in which this article should be read. Suppliers involved with the project have already indicated strong preparations for the upcoming irrigation season. With the success of these new strategies, the expectation is that the redemption rate will increase significantly in the upcoming irrigation season, allowing the project to achieve scale.

Box 7.1 Pointers to the creation of a sustainable market

Two demand surveys conducted by the project, independently from suppliers, to assess market changes reveal that farmers have not only appreciated the fact they have been able to acquire the technologies through a discount promotion but also that they have had direct contact with suppliers. Many who plan to upgrade their technologies in the near future noted that they now know exactly where to go to purchase these technologies. The experience improved productivity and increased production, and many noted that their capacity to buy these technologies at full price has been enhanced: 'I never knew I would acquire an efficient technology this year', 'I certainly plan to purchase another technology next year', 'In just one season, my production levels have increased significantly and should be able to upgrade to higher technologies' (some voices of farmers in Zambia).

The project started implementation in a very weak market for irrigation technologies. While the project is only through the first year of operation, there are positive signs of a growing market with changes in market dynamics beyond access to the targeted product or technology. Table 7.1 highlights some of the key results experienced to date.

Future success lies in proactive investments from the suppliers particularly in appropriate levels of inventory, business interactions with farmers and innovative and cost-effective direct marketing. The cost of reaching out to farmers has been an issue for most suppliers requiring innovation in marketing and distribution networks. While some private sector companies appreciate and are receptive to development programmes that are based on pure business principles, past interactions with development organizations that do not apply market development approaches mean it is hard to get suppliers to fully embrace their lead roles, often requiring push from the facilitating development organization.

Risks of vouchers

Despite the strong potential for this approach, there are some risks that need to be addressed when applying a voucher model:

- *Inadequate value chain analysis or market assessment prior to selecting the voucher model.* It is important that as part of the programme design process, due attention is paid to supply and demand issues to ensure that the voucher approach is the right model or appropriately structured.
- *Inappropriate voucher value.* If the value is not significant enough, the discount will not serve as an adequate incentive for farmers to try this technology. If the discount is too high, then the farmer no longer pays a realistic portion of the technology price.
- *The full-price of the technology is not affordable.* If the technology is not reasonably priced then the demand and market for technology once the voucher is withdrawn will not be sustained. The involvement of multiple suppliers has helped introduce competition meaning that prices are relatively affordable.

Table 7.1 Market development changes

Market aspect	Demand side	Supply side
Risk aversion	Growing number of farmers using own funds and vouchers to purchase the technologies	Suppliers investing in newer, quality inventory of the technologies
Seller–buyer interactions	Farmers' affirmation and appreciation of first-time interactions with suppliers	Suppliers' affirmation that selling technologies directly to farmers has brought realization that smallholder farmers can be direct customers of such agricultural technologies
	Farmers making informed buying decision and technology choices	
Client satisfaction	Farmers provided with warranty and are therefore able to ensure poor quality products are repaired in a timely manner	Suppliers and manufacturers switching frompoor quality to better quality technologies
Direct technology marketing	Farmers have gained exposure to all available technologies on market (previously did not have this opportunity)	Suppliers beginning to market technologies through agricultural fairs and technology demonstrations as well as setting up distribution networks
		Suppliers slowly embracing innovation in marketing and service provision
		Sales increased by more than 100% following implementation of water technology fairs, which provided farmers with an opportunity see and test the technology before purchase
Technology sales	Farmers who have successfully installed technologies are serving as a testimonial marketing to other farmers and leading to increased sales	From an annual average of 120 direct technology sales to nearly 500 direct technology sales to smallholder farmers in first five months of one irrigation season
		Suppliers previously mainly sold to NGOs; only5–10% was the portion of direct sales to smallholders
		Increase from one active supplier at the beginning of the voucher programme to four suppliers in five months
		Manufacturing and restocking now based ondirect effective demand by smallholder farmersnot NGO orders
Cost of technology	Farmers' choices of technologies reflective of the cost of technology; however, many showing enthusiasm for graduation to higher irrigation technologies	Sourcing of new technology suppliers and bulk orders pushing the prices of technology down
		Positive signals of reduced prices as increased competition and as suppliers seek new sourcesof suppliers of technologies
Technology performance and othe remerging impacts	Increased family participation in farming; motivated by presence of efficient technology	Local manufacturers responding tocompetingimported technologies and feedback from farmers

- *Leakage to non-target farmers.* The project has developed and applied an electronic Short-Messaging-System for voucher distribution and dissemination. The system incorporates a number of fraud prevention mechanisms to ensure the intent and integrity of the vouchers is upheld. To date, the programme has not witnessed any incidences of fraud. The use of these mechanisms (including distinct farmer identification numbers) and the incorporation of an SMS system prevent vouchers from having a cash value, other than for the purchase of a technology. Additionally, these technologies are better suited for smaller plot sizes; larger farmers self-select themselves out of the programme.
- *Failure to ensure adequate exit strategies* for the activities surrounding the voucher programme, such as agricultural fairs, that support the distribution and marketing of technologies. As MEDA enters the second year of implementation, strategies are being developed to download activities to the private sector. From the beginning of the project, this expectation was shared with project partners.
- *Limiting time duration.* The MEDA project will only run for three years. Given the initial reluctance of commercial suppliers to engage in marketing, it would have been ideal to run the project over a longer period.
- *Implicit handouts.* Even when building a commercial supply chain, there is the potential that NGOs can 'implicitly' insert themselves in the value chain by handling transportation or monitoring quality control. It was important that the project team avoided such activities.

Factors for sustainability

While the project is in its early days, the high level of direct sales to farmers and initial results reveal the potential of the programme to address farmers' risk aversion. Once positive behavioural change towards technology adoption is experienced, the vouchers can be removed leaving behind functioning supply chains. In order for this to occur, the Zambia project has highlighted some critical factors for success that will contribute to sustainability:

- *Be low-key.* One of the important messages that MEDA has conveyed to all stakeholders is that MEDA's role need not be highlighted. MEDA's name is not marked on the vouchers and the project vehicles do not have MEDA stickers. Instead, MEDA tries to ensure that farmers are aware that the promotion comes from the suppliers, not MEDA or its partners. This has been easier said than done as farmers often ask what MEDA's role is in the project. However, private sector companies have shown appreciation of this strategy as it puts them in the forefront.
- *Ensure that there is a range of competitors in the marketplace.* Farmers have the voucher to purchase either a treadle pump or drip irrigation kit. No supplier is promoted over another. A supplier's success is therefore dictated by their ability to serve farmers' demand with the best product and appropriate service.

- *Price is critical.* It is important to ensure that buyers – smallholder farmers in this case – know the real price of the subsidized product. The discount should be transparent. It is equally important that the discounted price does not vary widely from the real cost of the product.
- *Incorporate complementary activities as appropriate.* In very weak supply markets, as was the case in Zambia, the voucher may not be enough to stimulate the market. Complementary or corresponding supply-side interventions are sometimes necessary to demonstrate the business case to private sector companies before their full engagement. This is usually the case when private sector actors are sceptical about the profitability and viability of servicing smallholder farmers or the market has significantly been distorted by free products. Such supply-side interventions may include awareness on retail network development or support for innovative marketing strategies.
- *Find strategies to highlight the demonstration effects.* Smallholder farmers who are able to substantially increase their incomes as a result of a treadle pump or drip irrigation system are the best promoter of the product. Using successful farmers as model farmers will be critical to ensuring that the demand for these technologies is sustained over the long term.
- *Ensure that the vouchers are time bound.* In the case of Zambia, each certificate has one-year validity. The voucher programme will only operate for three years – after which the discounts will be withdrawn.
- *Develop long-term complementary solutions.* A critical factor for success of the voucher model in Zambia is the development of financial services. MEDA is also working with local financial institutions to develop their capacity in agricultural lending. Once the voucher has stimulated demand for these technologies and suppliers have invested in a retail network, farmers will be able to access the financial products that facilitate their purchase of these technologies. Finance is the long-term solution but it is not the sole solution if demand and retail networks are not developed.

Conclusion

MEDA's project in Zambia highlights how a voucher approach is being used to catalyse a sustainable supply chain for much-needed agricultural technologies. The programme's facilitation of commercial distribution systems aims to ensure sustainability of benefits for clients and other farming households after the project ends. Through stimulating the private sector (including technology demand and supply), MEDA's project will promote buyer–seller relationships that will enhance market relationships and interaction. The voucher approach and its role in market development still have critics. However, MEDA's project in Zambia is demonstrating that when properly designed with appropriate measures for sustainability, a voucher programme can act as an effective market stimulant. The experience in this voucher programme also shows that smart subsidies serve as stimulants for gradual market developments in weak markets that have been distorted by handouts. The ability to effect multiple market changes from a single market catalyst affirms the strength of well-designed market stimulants.

About the author

Alexandra Snelgrove (ASnelgrove@meda.org) is the Project Manager/Senior Consultant, Production and Marketing Linkages, MEDA (Mennonite Economic Development Associates) and **Lemmy Manje** is the Field Project Manager Zambia, Production and Marketing Linkages, MEDA (Mennonite Economic Development Associates).

References

Frausto, K. (2000) 'Developing irrigation options for small farmers', report prepared for World Commission on Dams, International Development Enterprises, Denver, USA.

Government of Zambia (2002) *Poverty Reduction Strategy Paper*, Government of Zambia, Lusaka.

Government of Zambia (2006) *Poverty Reduction Strategy Paper*, Government of Zambia, Lusaka.

Gregory, I. (2006) 'The role of input vouchers in pro-poor growth', background paper, African Fertilizer Summit, 9–13 June 2006, Abuja, Nigeria

Hallberg, K. (2006) 'A retrospective assessment of the Kenya Voucher Training Programme,' *Small Enterprise Development* 17 (2): 56–67.

Hichaambwa, M. and Tschirley, D. (2006) *Understanding Zambia's Domestic Value Chains for Fresh Fruit and Vegetables*, Food Security Research Project, Michigan State University, Michigan.

McVay, M. and Miehlbradt, A. (2006) *Implementing Sustainable Private Sector Development: Striving for Tangible Results for the Poor?*, International Training Centre, International Labour Organization, Turin.

UNDP (United Nations Development Program) (2008) *UN Human Development Report – Going Beyond Income*, UNDP [online] http://hdrstats.undp.org/2008/countries/country_fact_sheets/cty_fs_ZMB.html [accessed 26 January 2009].

World Bank (2005) 'Project performance assessment report', Kenya Micro and Small Enterprise Training and Technology Project, Sector, Thematic, and Global Evaluation Group Operations Evaluation Department, World Bank, Washington DC.

CHAPTER 8

Bringing together push and pull through local entrepreneurs

Sally Walkerman, Michael Bowles, Trinnie Cartland and Sally Ross

Abstract

Despite significant efforts in agriculture market development, millions of smallholder farmers remain isolated from markets, due to remoteness and low farm productivity. Push/pull approaches to market development suggest a dual strategy for bringing smallholders into agricultural markets: 1) reduce producer vulnerability and build capacities, based on market requirements; and 2) facilitate relationships for producers to deal in consistent, growing markets. While simple in concept and effective as an approach, the execution of push/pull is complex. In particular, it is difficult to connect push (producer capacity) and pull (market) elements, resulting in unsustainable market linkages. When applying a push/pull approach in areas where the Aga Khan Foundation (AKF) works, AKF has noted that local entrepreneurs can link push and pull effectively and for the long term. This case study reviews how entrepreneurs link push and pull in AKF's market development programme in southern Tanzania. It outlines learning on how local entrepreneurs bridge gaps between producers and firms, taking the case of remote farmers accessing inputs (seed, fertilizer, implements, and pesticide) from larger suppliers. The paper describes the challenge of linking push and pull, outlines AKF's experience in southern Tanzania, and follows with points for discussion on incorporating local entrepreneurs into push/pull programmes.

Keywords: entrepreneurship, agriculture, value chains, market development

It is widely held that smallholder farmers are vital to economic growth and sustainable agriculture. Well-trained and well-organized smallholders generate livelihoods for themselves and respond well to market needs, as noted by Altieri and Koohafkan (2008), and widely by FAO (2014) and IFAD (2011). In addition, recent studies, including lipton (2012) and Bravo-Ortega and Lederman (2005), have shown that small farms are more efficient users of resources, are good drivers of innovation, and generate more output, employment, and income per hectare than large farms. This suggests that improvements in smallholder agricultural productivity and the integration of small-scale into markets can have dramatic implications for rural employment, food security, and broader economic growth. However, integrating small-scale

http://dx.doi.org/10.3362/9781780448879.008

producers into markets remains challenging in most development contexts, due to a host of interconnected factors including remoteness, unstable for demand and supply of products, inconsistent market information, and low on-farm productivity.

Push/pull approaches are employed to help develop strong, pro-poor markets that buy effectively and efficiently from smallholders, and supply producers with adequate inputs at fair costs. With push/pull frameworks, facilitators pursue two parallel strategies, which this paper defines as follows: push builds producer capacities, based on market requirements; and pull encourages the integration of producers into markets. Push is necessary to undertake so that private firms can enter a geographic area. It typically involves increasing farmer knowledge on production techniques and improving producers' processes and facilities for harvest, post-harvest bulking, and storing, tailored to fit market needs, so that the firm can work with well-organized producers. Pull can involve a range of interventions aimed at improving producers' options for participating in markets. This may include increasing the capacity of actors who are aggregating or bulking produce to meet buyer requirements, integrating production of low-input or short season crops to increase incomes quickly, and facilitating the entry of 'lead firms' that view the area as a market for their products (agro-inputs) or source of needed raw materials.

For the purpose of this case study, we focus on pull approaches that facilitate the entry of lead firms. We define lead firms as stable businesses that can offer inputs and services, absorb produce, add value, pay fair prices, generate employment, and grow the sector. A lead firm can be built within the programme's geographical area, or headquartered outside the area and encouraged to expand into it (the type, business structure, and location are dependent on context). We focus on lead firms because implementation experience has revealed that lead firms' involvement in setting the programme approach and their active participation is critical to success.

When it comes to remote, smallholder producers, there is typically a wide gap between farm and market. While push/pull programmes aim to reduce this gap, challenges exist to sustain the link between producer and firm. The next section will outline the gaps between producers and firms and will describe some of the challenges that emerge when trying to link them together.

Challenge of integrating push/pull methodologies

There is significant complexity in developing strong, sustainable links between push and pull elements (see USAID's call for practitioner learning; SEEP Network, 2014). When applying a push/pull approach in several countries where the Aga Khan Foundation (AKF) works, programme staff found that there is rarely a direct, natural link between producer and lead firm. For the producer, there is a lack of volume (often the case even with a farmers' group), lack of time, and often a lack of interest in developing deep or long-term direct relationships with a company. at the same time, companies are rarely able to deal directly with large numbers of fragmented smallholder farmers.

In between producers and firms, therefore, lies a gap in communication, commitment, and trust that can undermine inclusive market development. this gap is especially wide in rural and remote areas, where private sector activity and producer connections are low. This gap can undermine opportunities for the scale, and especially the sustainability of a programme.

Push/pull programmes have experimented with a range of options to develop links between producers and firms to address the gap. These options include organizing farmers' groups or cooperatives to purchase inputs in bulk and sell produce in larger quantities, encouraging firms to operate more vertically along the value chain, such as by expanding into input provision on contract, and by developing agent inter mediaries between producers and firms. These have been used, for example, in the 'LEAD' programme in Uganda and the 'AGENT' programme in Zimbabwe (World Bank, 2005). In implementing market development programmes in remote areas, AKF has seen opportunities in which local entrepreneurs can play key roles as agents in linking producers (or producers' groups) and firms.

The value of local entrepreneurs in linking value chain actors

While every context demands unique tactics and models, AKF's experience suggests that local entrepreneurs can play a central role in most cases of connecting producers and lead firms in market development. This paper posits that independent local entrepreneurs are effective intermediaries between smallholder farmers and firms in push/pull programmes, and have market-oriented incentives to play this role, which can enhance sustainability. With short-term support, they can be effective links over the long term.

This section outlines the qualities of and incentives for local entrepreneurs to be effective bridges between the two groups. We define local entrepreneurs as individuals who are based in the local area, who are business-minded and active in their own community. Their business orientation increases the likelihood that they are able to build and maintain working relationships with lead firms who need business-oriented local partners. They are also deeply aware of their community's context, challenges, opportunities, and issues, and, as noted in Loveridge and Schaeffer (2000), are able to tailor offerings accordingly. Finally, they have the right incentives to develop mutually beneficial relationships along their portion of the value chain, as these grow their business. Local entrepreneurs can therefore:

- intermediate between producers and firms;
- channel inputs to producers in hard-to-reach areas;
- negotiate contextually appropriate deals for buying and selling;
- organize smallholders to aggregate produce;

- help enforce compliance with contracts and standards; and
- deliver essential market information between actors.

Local entrepreneurs' incentives are aligned to play these roles, as each can be leveraged into a business line for them. They do this by developing different types of long-term relationships between themselves, firms, and rural producers, so they can sell value-added services to both and turn these services into viable businesses for themselves.

Their placement in the system also helps serve significant development goals. For example, where a programme would struggle to reach remote areas consistently and comprehensively, a local entrepreneur may have a business incentive and the connections required. This is especially interesting where government extension services are limited and farmers can rely on advice from a trusted input supplier or trader. Where government extension agents are focused on production alone, local entrepreneurs can provide marketing information and advice on possible opportunities, as noted in Ferris et al. (2014).

How entrepreneurs emerge and fill gaps between producers and firms will depend largely on the context. The next section outlines one case in which local entrepreneurship helped to connect producers and firms in the context of southern Tanzania's rice and sesame producers. In the case study, we explain how AKF identified the specific challenge in linking push and pull elements, how local entrepreneurs were strengthened to bridge the gap, and how they were identified and supported. The section that follows outlines lessons learned and points for discussion on the case.

Tanzania case

Background to the case

Lindi and Mtwara regions of Tanzania are some of the most economically and socially isolated regions of the country. Agricultural extension officers cover an average of 3,000 producers each; social services, including schooling and health care, are well below national averages; and key poverty indicators are among the worst in the country. When AKF started working there in 2009, agricultural productivity was at one half of the country's averages for most staple crops. Input supply was inconsistent, with some inputs provided through a poorly functioning government voucher system and very low market availability of inputs.

AKF's Coastal Rural Support Program, Tanzania [CRSP(T)] was started in 2009 with a mission to improve quality of life in Lindi and Mtwara regions through interventions in economic as well as social sectors. With financial support from the UK department for International Development, CRSP(T) started a programme to support farmers to increase production of rice and sesame and to facilitate better integration into markets. The project has parallel push strategies to build local agricultural production, organization, and extension systems, and pull strategies to encourage lead firms (end-market actors and input suppliers) to enter the target area.

Implementation approach

CRSP(T) started with multiple push activities designed to increase famers' capacity, production, and links to markets, as well as pull activities to bring in private firms. This section outlines the approach and identifies specific activities that evolved when a key gap was identified between producers and firms.

Push activities for CRSP(T) involve direct training and broad extension messaging, including radio, to boost the uptake of good agricultural practices and intensification methods. Producers are trained on farming methods that improve yields but require low external input costs and support water conservation and soil nutrition, and are encouraged to track their progress. Push activities also leverage early yield gains to realize improved incomes by organizing collective storage and sale when prices are high. In the same geographical areas, CRSP(T) also supports push through its Community-Based Savings Group programme, which is reducing household vulnerability by providing a safe place to save money and take small loans.

Pull activities involve developing relationships with upstream and downstream actors, particularly national and international buyers and input suppliers. This involves capacity building of primary cooperative societies (PCSs) as conduits for buyers, piloting contract farming with lead firms (e.g. Export Trading Group), exposure visits for small business-holders to encourage investments in better post-processing equipment and storage facilities, and encouraging input suppliers (e.g. Yara, Minjingu, Balton, East African Seed Company, etc.) to expand their businesses in the area to increase market availability of inputs.

By the mid-point of this six-year project, CRSP(T) had trained just over 33,000 farmers, rice yields were increasing (some 2–3 times), and farmers were starting to experience increased incomes from selling their rice and sesame. However, the supply chain for inputs remained a major issue.

The original approach for improving the availability of inputs was to encourage PCSs to supply inputs to members on a fee basis, as a farm shop would in more developed areas, and to encourage lead firm input suppliers to visit the region to scope out possible expansion with the PCSs as delivery channels. However, the project experienced limited uptake. PCS leadership and farmers were not well-aligned to take up the system, because of capacity constraints, lack of trust, and lack of PCS interest in developing relationships with private input suppliers. Lead input supply firms found they could not develop productive relationships with the PCSs due to lack of management capacity at the PCSs, and they could not develop a strong business case to sell direct-to-producer with such dispersed and small clients.

For the programme, the original approach was clearly insufficient. Staff knew that if farmers continued without a reliable source of fertilizer, implements, seed, pesticide, and other services, the increased production experienced with the push activities would be temporary.

CRSP(T) decided to change tactics to unlock the barriers to entry for supplying inputs. The programme started training local entrepreneurial individuals as village-based agents (VBAs), who would set up their own small businesses to channel inputs from larger firms, divide them into smaller quantities, and provide them at appropriate prices to producers. CRSP(T) chose this change after seeing that cooperative-oriented and group-oriented players lacked the business acumen to grow on their own or be sustainable.

Activities supporting local entrepreneurs

CRSP(T) identified the gap between input suppliers and producers at the outset of the project, but the programme's first attempt to link these via primary cooperative societies was unsuccessful. The idea to address the gap through entrepreneurs came from looking at private sector-driven models that had been successful in other sectors and geographical areas.

Programme staff worked to identify, train, and support local entrepreneurs through the following activities:

- *Identification.* Staff living and working in the programme's target communities sought participants who were already active as business people, or those who demonstrated entrepreneurial qualities such as interest in leadership positions in farmers' groups, understanding of finance, and creativity in problem solving. Most of these were already farmers, and thus experienced in the requirements of seeking inputs and selling produce.
- *Training.* In groups of 30–50, local entrepreneurs gathered with programme staff and representatives from input supply companies. They were trained over an initial 3–5 day period on topics of financial record-keeping, methods for managing an input supply business, and about the products, their safe use, and proper storage.
- *Support.* In the beginning, CRSP(T) staff worked with VBAs to build trust between them and the input supply companies. VBAs were encouraged to adopt mobile money payment so that companies could be sure of receiving a partial pre-payment for their products, which helped the supply chain to start flowing. As VBAs have gained experience and started growing their businesses, CRSP(T) has provided refresher training (including for some VBAs' staff) and other linkages to new companies and technologies. To assist smaller VBAs who are still developing their ability to identify and exploit new opportunities, CRSP(T) provides opportunities for VBAs to go on exposure visits to other parts of Tanzania where markets function more effectively, and highlights new products or technologies that VBAs can offer. One member of CRSP(T) staff is in charge of training and identifying areas of support for VBAs. He visits a selection of VBAs on a regular basis to gather data on their progress and to hear about issues or bottlenecks they are experiencing. Decisions about whether to help with an issue are made by CRSP(T) management, depending on whether: 1) the problem can be adequately addressed within the current project; 2) CRSP(T) helping to solve the problem will have a long-term impact; and 3) there isn't another actor already operating in the value chain who could solve the issue instead.

Results

Nearly 200 VBAs have been trained through the programme, with roughly a third developing strong, profitable businesses. Different VBAs operate with different sizes and growth trajectories for their companies. Some have become small enterprises with several staff and formal agro-input shops. Others operate on a mobile basis, serving dispersed farmers in remote areas by bicycle or motorbike. Farmers use the VBAs as input suppliers because they can access what they need much closer to home, rather than investing in travelling to urban centres. Most VBAs report that they advise farmers on appropriate inputs as a key part of their business and that they get quick feedback from farmers if they have suggested the wrong product. In this way, VBAs are held accountable when necessary. Profits range from US$50 to $3,000 per quarter per active VBA.

Over time, these entrepreneurs have started, on their own, organizing themselves both horizontally and vertically to coordinate supply, sales, and training (see Figure 8.1). Horizontal organization has come in the form of VBAs teaming up together to purchase inputs in bulk at a lower per-unit cost than they would be able to receive individually. As a group they have also invested in training for certification on the handling of chemicals, which is a requirement for distributing pesticide in Tanzania. This leads naturally to providing spraying services to farmers, which is described in Box 8.1. Some VBAs are also providing advice to farmers on agronomic practices, in addition to supplying inputs. CRSP(T) has been working with VBAs to encourage them to assess and take up new service/ revenue streams.

Vertically, the programme has seen several VBAs build larger businesses in less remote areas. They are more closely linked to the lead firms, and less closely linked to the producers. To reach producers, they have started selling into more remote areas through VBAs based rurally, who have close access to producers and operate on a smaller scale.

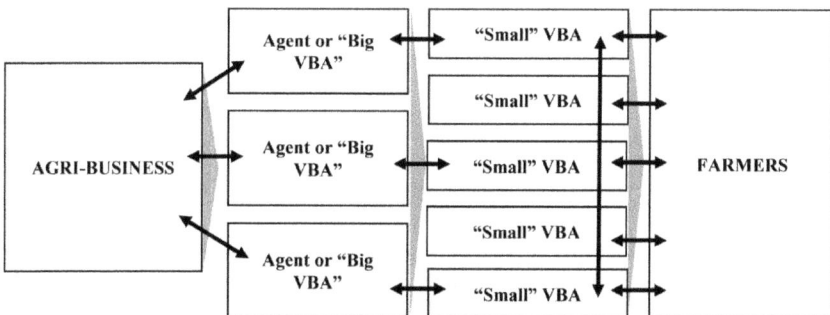

Figure 8.1 Vertical and horizontal integration of VBAs

Box 8.1 Value-added services: spray teams

Local entrepreneurs can improve their business models by diversifying products and services. With training and encouragement from CRSP(T), a fifth of active VBAs offer spraying services to their customers. VBAs assemble and train small teams of people to visit a farmer's field to spray pesticide. This has significant advantages, including:

- Farmers pay for the service and only the amount of pesticide used on their crops, reducing *cost to them and removing the need to store pesticide at home.*
- Trained people are spraying, and are more likely to use appropriate techniques and protective equipment.
- VBAs are able to increase their revenue streams that take advantage of training (in chemical handling), in which they have already invested.

When it became clear to CRSP(T) that innovations were occurring between the trained entrepreneurs, programme management chose to start developing support activities in response to steps taken by the entrepreneurs. Now, programme activities are dedicated to intervention areas that are already being tried by entrepreneurs and thus have buy-in already. For example, the entrepreneurs decided to formalize themselves as an association, to increase credibility in the Tanzanian context and to provide a platform through which lead firms can channel bulk sales. CRSP(T) has assisted the entrepreneurs with navigating the registration process and has advised them on options for formalizing.

With a stronger link to the programme area via VBAs, input supply companies have become willing to invest in demonstration plots in the programme area, which improve farmers' understanding of how various inputs work, encouraging greater demand for inputs and therefore supporting greater firm activity. CRSP(T) is helping by encouraging the demo plots, but is encouraging the lead input firms to work independently as well. As the VBA system grows, CRSP(T) will continue looking for ways in which the programme, or private firms, can support the entrepreneurship already happening in the field.

This approach is unlocking benefits for rural producers and entrepreneurs, but significant challenges remain. While the VBAs have worked as a model for developing distribution channels for inputs, larger vulnerabilities to market failure are significant. In particular, the VBAs struggle with access to the right level of finance. Further intervention in the geographic area is needed by financial institutions to offer creative solutions to this issue.

Discussion points

Many market development programmes include (or are based around) entrepreneurship. Cultivating entrepreneurial qualities is the main thrust of 'farming as a business' methodologies, advanced by facilitators to teach farmers to operate more like a formal business in their work. Critical elements involve seeking and using market information to make choices about cropping techniques, timing, and location of sale; quantifying costs and returns; and linking as closely as possible to the end-market in order to derive maximum value from produce. While these skills for a producer are critical, the profile of an entrepreneur linking producers and lead firms is slightly different. Based on AKF's experience, entrepreneurs capable of interfacing between producers and lead firms need a combination of the qualities listed below in order to have a good chance for success in connecting push and pull elements. The key qualities identified are:

- *Deep understanding of the local context.* For lead firms coming from outside a remote area, the most critical issue they face is a lack of understanding of local tastes, needs, constraints, access points, and distribution channels. Entrepreneurs developed from the local community are most likely to contain this knowledge. An added advantage here is that those who enter business in their local area are more likely to be bound by norms to act in good faith, and are more likely to remain long-term players.
- *Credibility with producers.* In AKF's experience, entrepreneurs who are going to link value chain components together need to have the respect and trust of local producers. Those who are, or were at one time, farmers from the target area themselves have been more successful in the Tanzanian case outlined above.
- *Demonstrated leadership and business orientation.* It is widely accepted that some individuals are more business-oriented, with an interest in self-employment, are comfortable marketing themselves, and have a higher tolerance for risk. These people may not necessarily have a new idea to take to the market but they are able to identify opportunities, experiment in their work, and learn new skills through trial and error. Often, they are slightly better educated or may have relatives who operate businesses, which helps them understand the risks and opportunities on a deep level.

AKF has also found that supporting entrepreneurs is a delicate balance, where too little or too much (or the wrong type) undermines sustainability. In this regard, AKF's experience to date has shown that support could be understood to follow these general steps: 1) push first; 2) engage lead firms; and 3) follow the entrepreneurs, as outlined below.

Push first

In most cases in AKF's programme areas, significant push efforts (tailored to needs outlined by key lead firms) are required before lead firms are interested in becoming active. These are typically remote areas where producers are dispersed and unaware of market demands or opportunities. Push activities to increase production, enhance farmers' understanding of market demands, reduce post-harvest losses (and improve post-harvest handling), and improve farming households' resilience to unexpected shocks, are necessary for lead firms to be able to invest in extending their business to the programme area. This sequencing of 'push first' requires facilitators to work with lead firms to develop the most appropriate interventions, to keep their lead firm partners updated and jointly monitor progress, and to support the lead firms to increase activities in the programme area at the point when the lead firms see that production volumes, quality, and aggregation efficiencies allow them to do so for business reasons.

Engage lead firms

When push activities start to show results, it would be expected that lead firms start to take serious interest in the area. They may outline issues that remain even when production improves. While some issues will be appropriate for a facilitator, other firm, or government to address, some will be natural points to probe to see if a local entrepreneur (or entrepreneurs) might be able to resolve them. At this point, different programmes take different tacks for developing entrepreneurs. For example, the AGENT programme in Zimbabwe involved an NGO that aggregated orders for inputs on behalf of all the entrepreneurs, and placed bulk orders with large firms for two years – acting directly within the marketplace. AKF's approach, outlined in the previous section, limits the NGO role to making and supporting firm–entrepreneur connections.

Following the entrepreneurs

Once entrepreneurs are in place, a programme can watch and support steps taken by them as they evolve their business offerings and confront challenges. This requires close, on-the-ground contact with the entrepreneurs. While dependent on context, criteria can be developed and applied to understand how to support entrepreneurs as a facilitating organization. AKF tends to limit support as noted above to advising, connecting, and training/exposing actors to opportunities; however, different contexts may require more or less, or different types of involvement.

This section has outlined a general framework for how entrepreneurs might work within a push/pull programme to address gaps between producers and lead firms. It is important to recognize that this framework is suggested for remote areas, where entrepreneurs would be encouraged to participate alongside other activities improving push and pull aspects. Without organized farmers or lead firms willing to link up, the chances of success for entrepreneurs would be limited.

Conclusion

The purpose of undertaking this extended review of entrepreneurship in a particular push/pull context was to gather learning on the challenge of linking push and pull aspects, and to understand how a new role can be encouraged in the value chain to address linkage gaps. In the case study above, CRSP(T) supported entrepreneurs to take up activities that were strong business opportunities but that did not exist before the push activities were implemented. In doing so, the programme catalysed a new value chain channel, which is expected to continue in the long term. While the entrepreneurs will continue to experience a diverse set of challenges including lack of access to finance, vulnerability to market failure, and uncertainty with regard to political-economic policies, so far, it appears that these entrepreneurs will remain in place and profitable.

For the development community, a key question coming out of this experience is 'can it scale?' Bringing market development programmes to scale is a perennial challenge, with many interventions being too seated within their local context to be appropriate for expansion. In the case of this learning, it is expected that the concept can be replicated, if tailored to its specific context. However, AKF's experience is that training and mentoring of the entrepreneurs on business basics and new opportunities is needed (whether undertaken by private firm or non-profit), making it unlikely that such efforts would be taken up without any support at all. Even further, experience shows that significant push activities are needed with farmers and pull activities are needed with lead firms to prepare the ground for local entrepreneurs to initiate business activities in the value chain: farmers need to be aware of opportunities and tactics for increasing their yield and accessing markets, and lead firms need to be aware of the opportunity to trade in the geographic area and be willing to engage. Otherwise, the business environment will not be ready for the local entrepreneur's offering in the value chain.

Supporting entrepreneurship at the interface of push and pull can help increase the long-term effects of push/pull programmes in different contexts, especially in extremely remote areas where there are few existing incentives for firms to engage. In this way, there is potential for local entrepreneurs to address the last-mile problem for firms, and for producers to gain stronger, long-term access to supplies and markets.

About the authors

Sally Walkerman (sally.walkerman@akdn.org) is Senior Programme Officer for rural development at the Aga Khan Foundation in Tanzania, where she oversees strategy and partnerships for enterprise, agriculture and market development in Tanzania. **Michael Bowles** (mike.bowles@akdn.org) leads market development programming for Aga Khan Foundation globally and is based in Geneva, Switzerland. **Trinnie Cartland** (trinnie.cartland@akfea.org) is an agriculture and market development professional and manager of the Aga Khan Foundation's Food Security & Incomes programme in southeastern Tanzania. **Sally Ross** (sally.ross@akfea.org) is an agribusiness professional and Monitoring, Evaluation, Action Research and Communications Manager with Aga Khan Foundation Tanzania.

References

Sltieri, M.A. and Koohafkan, P. (2008) *Enduring Farms: Climate Change, Smallholders and Traditional Farming Communities* [pdf], Third World Network, Environment & Development Series 6 <www.fao.org/nr/water/docs/enduring_Farms.pdf> [accessed 6 January 2015].

Bravo-Ortega, C. and Lederman, d. (2005) *Agriculture and National Welfare Around the World: Causality and International Heterogeneity Since 1960* [pdf], World Bank Policy Research Working Paper 3499, February 2005 <http://elibrary.worldbank.org/doi/book/10.1596/1813-9450-3499> [accessed 6 January 2015].

Ferris, S., Robbins, P., Best, R., Seville, D., Buxton, A., Shriver, J., and Wei, E. (2014) *Linking Smallholder Farmers to Markets and the Implications for Extension and Advisory Services*, MEAS Discussion Paper 4 <www.value-chains.org/dyn/bds/docs/871/MEAS%20Discussion%20Paper%204%20-%20Linking%20Farmers%20to%20Mar.pdf> [accessed 6 January 2015].

Food and Agriculture Organization (2014) *State of Food Insecurity in the World 2014* [online], FAO <www.fao.org/publications/sofi/2014/en/> [accessed 6 January 2015].

International Fund for Agricultural Development (2011) *View Point: Smallholders Can Feed the World* [pdf], IFAD <www.ifad.org/pub/viewpoint/smallholder.pdf> [accessed 6 January 2015].

Lipton, M. (2012) *Income from Work: The Food–Population–Resource Crisis in the 'Short Africa'* [pdf], Leontief Prize Lecture, Tufts University, Medford, MA, 3 April 2012 <www.ase.tufts.edu/gdae/about_us/Leontief/LiptonleontiefPrizeComments.pdf> [accessed 6 January 2015].

Loveridge, S. and Schaeffer, P.V. (2000) *Small Town and Rural Economic Development: A Case Studies Approach*, Westport, CT: Praeger.

SEEP Network (2014) 'USAID calls for practitioner learning from push/pull and inclusive market development' [blog], SEEP Network, February 2014 <www.seepnetwork.org/blog/leo-call-project-examples-inclusive-market-development-2> [accessed 15 January 2015].

World Bank (2005) 'Zimbabwe: AGENT Program', in World Bank, *Agriculture Investment Sourcebook* [pdf], Washington, DC: World Bank <https://openknowledge.worldbank.org/handle/10986/7308> [accessed 11 January 2015].

CHAPTER 9

Making markets work for women: how push and pull strategies can support women's economic empowerment

*Christine Faveri, Kerry Jane Wilson
and Perveen Shaikh*

Abstract

In many countries, the inability of women to negotiate pervasive social, legal, and cultural barriers inhibits their participation in the productive sphere, particularly their entry into market systems as producers and entrepreneurs. The paper draws on case studies from projects implemented by the Mennonite Economic Development Associates (MEDA) in Ghana, the Entrepreneurship and Community Development Institute (ECDI) in Pakistan, and Zardozi in Afghanistan to show how practitioners can maximize 'push' and 'pull' strategies to increase the scale, impact, and sustainability of women's economic empowerment programming. Despite differences in country contexts, value chains, and sectors, the authors illustrate the importance of 'push' strategies in helping women to overcome the persistent gender-based discrimination that undermines women's understanding of markets, access to networks, self-confidence, and business success. They also show how deliberate 'pull' strategies that use commercially based incentives can increase women's incomes and business sustainability. The authors conclude that a blend of push and pull strategies will provide the most reach and impact for women's economic empowerment projects, ensuring income growth and gender equality dividends for families and communities.

Keywords: women's economic empowerment, market systems development, Ghana, Afghanistan, Pakistan

Gender inequality has been defined as a binding constraint that affects inclusive market system development around the world (De Santos, 2013). For several years, the United Nations has underscored the multiplier effect that investing in women and girls can have on productivity, efficiency, and sustained economic growth. The private sector is increasingly recognizing that equitable inclusion of women in formal employment can increase GDP significantly in many regions of the world (Goldman Sachs and JB Were, 2009).

In turn, there is evidence that reducing poverty can increase women's economic empowerment. However, women's access to economic resources cannot

http://dx.doi.org/10.3362/9781780448879.009

be considered an end in itself. For women to be economically empowered, they must have the ability and choice to make and act on economic decisions (Golla et al., 2011). Academics and policymakers concerned about women's economic empowerment and inclusive gender equitable growth, have learned that effective and sustainable development programming must be grounded in a strong understanding of the specific and localized environments in which programmes operate. Women's economic empowerment alone may not lead to gender equality (Jones, 2012). A multiplicity of context-specific variables will determine the transformative potential of paid work (Kabeer et al., 2011).

Feminist theory and practice have underscored the importance of recognizing the social, class, and gender-specific rules and norms that order and shape relations between women and men, and between women themselves, in both the public and the private sphere. Market systems thinking is now acknowledging how gender analysis can help to identify the change points in a system that will facilitate a positive shift in women's ability to act and interact with complex market systems and subsystems (Markel and Jones, 2014).

Practitioners can use such learning to develop strategies to help women to move into markets ('push' strategies) and to encourage market actors to use commercial incentives to engage women producers and actors ('pull' strategies).

This chapter looks at how push and pull strategies have been used by three non-governmental organizations in different country contexts to facilitate market systems changes benefiting women: in the tailoring and embroidery sector in Afghanistan; hand-embellished fabrics in Pakistan; and the soybean value chain in northern Ghana. It shows how 'push' strategies will remain essential where women are severely culturally isolated but that the push-to-pull ratio can increase as certain pre-requisites are in place: women's business skills, networks, trust between market actors, and a proven business case for working with women. Finally, the authors show how 'push' and 'pull' can optimize scale, reach, and impact in terms of women's economic empowerment.

Using push and pull to support women's economic empowerment in Afghanistan, Pakistan and Ghana

Facilitating inclusive market systems development requires a number of strategies and interventions to catalyse system-level changes. USAid has referred to some of these strategies as 'push' and 'pull' strategies, particularly when describing market systems development programming (Seep Network, 2014):

- *Push strategies* are designed to help very poor individuals and households build up a minimum level of assets (e.g. human, financial, social, cultural) that increases their capability to engage with other market actors (both public and private) and transition out of a cycle of extreme poverty. Interventions may build household assets; improve linkages to social protection; build livelihood and 'market readiness' skills; improve 'soft' skills such as confidence, negotiating, or relationship building;

address chronic or temporary deficiencies in consumption; or strengthen household capacity to manage risk.

- *Pull strategies* leverage commercial incentives to facilitate the more gainful participation of the poor in economic opportunities so they can continue to improve their well-being beyond a project's life through sustained engagement in market systems – be it as a producer, labourer, employee, or business owner. Interventions may create less risky entry points or lower barriers to market entry.

In all parts of the world, gender inequality complicates access to finance, mobility, literacy, negotiation power, business registration, confidence, and trust between market actors. This is particularly true in religious or culturally conservative communities in countries such as Afghanistan and Pakistan where women's interactions are strictly moderated by family members; there is an insecure/conflict environment; and there are gendered rules and norms of the institutions with which women engage. However, even in middle-income countries, like Ghana, women's involvement in the economic sphere can be invisible and therefore go unsupported in economic development initiatives. For example, in northern Ghana, women in rural areas are primary contributors to the local economy as unpaid subsistence farm labour, but are rarely regarded as farmers.

A contextual understanding of how women and men interact in their communities; the roles that women play in the productive and reproductive sphere; and the social and cultural barriers and opportunities to women's full participation in market systems are critical to designing strategies that will maximize outcomes for women.

Zardozi: Markets for Afghan Women

Zardozi is a registered Afghan non-governmental organization (NGO) that has provided marketing support services to home-bound Afghan women embroiderers since 1984. In 2008, Zardozi shifted from a direct service delivery model to one of market facilitation to help raise incomes for poor, uneducated women through a commercially sustainable system which links female producers working in the informal economy to local markets. Zardozi works in four urban and semi-urban areas of Afghanistan: Kabul, Mazar, Herat, and Jalalabad.

Zardozi's Markets for Afghan Artisans project, jointly funded by the united Kingdom's department for international development and Oxfam Novib (2009–2015), was designed to overcome the shortcomings of traditional economic development projects for women in Afghanistan that have focused on vocational training without solid market analysis and the expansion of women in the formal sector. Through market research, Zardozi discovered that traditional business lines for women, such as tailoring and embroidery, were still able to absorb a significant amount of new business and thus began their work by focusing on connecting women already active in these sectors to new market opportunities.

In Afghanistan, supporting women to succeed in the informal sector is important given cultural and security constraints on women's mobility. Zardozi typically works with women in two major categories: those who are permitted by their families to engage in market activities with men; and those who have permission to operate a business only within the confines of their home or community.

Zardozi models itself as a business support network for women, providing them with membership in a credible organization that backs their businesses, new and advanced skills training, market research and information, and linkages with buyers. They work with skilled women who are committed to starting a business and focus on helping them to build their markets and social networks. In Afghanistan, this is critically important as men's business support networks are embedded in trust-based extended family relations. Business networks facilitate access to credit, inputs, buyers, and distribution channels for goods. Because women are not valued or perceived as potential business partners, they are routinely excluded.

Zardozi's use of push and pull strategies in Afghanistan

Many of the strategies that Zardozi employs to reach and support women can be termed 'push' strategies. For NGOs operating in Afghanistan, this is a critical first step in reaching and mobilizing Afghan women, many of whom are extremely poor, illiterate, and isolated. Zardozi's clients take tremendous risks to cross cultural barriers to earn an income.

A traditional 'push' strategy implemented by Zardozi has been the provision of basic business and skills training to women working in the informal garment sector. The entry point is training around new designs for sewing and beadwork products – socially and culturally acceptable activities that women can undertake in their homes. The 'push' from Zardozi comes in the provision of basic equipment (cutting table, scissors, or sewing machine) and product samples as required. What are atypical, in Afghanistan, are Zardozi's next steps. After the initial training, women are provided with intensive business training and then linked directly to a market or buyer, ideally within six weeks. A full cycle of the programme would see a woman mentored through the production of at least one order for a product.

Once women are successful in understanding the process and committed to continuing their businesses, Zardozi encourages them to join their network. This is a membership-based organization where they can receive ongoing business services (design, marketing, quality control, branding, and packaging) for a small fee. The services are delivered through Zardozi's Community Business Centres (CBCs) (67 in total) located in women's houses. Set up as women-only safe spaces, the CBCs are located within walking distance of 30 to 35 group members and are connected to one of four registered Nisfe Jahan or guilds that function as a community-level business association for women. The Nisfe Jahan is now registered with the Ministry of Justice. There are four branches (Herat, Mazar, Jalalabad, and Kabul) in the process of federating and establishing links with other similar associations such as Afghan Women's Business Federation, Afghan Women's Business Council, and Afghan Women's Network. Through the CBC, Zardozi facilitates linkages for women with local banks and promotes participation in local savings groups and traditional rotating savings and credit associations, where available. The CBCs encourage women to engage in flexible diverse business opportunities, e.g. moving from sewing to also raising chickens to sell eggs. They also provide social/peer support, build confidence and aspiration for business, allow women to cope with change, and stay connected to an informal market place that has very few opportunities for women.

In Afghanistan, 'pull' strategies to stimulate women's economic empowerment are more limited and challenging to employ. Due to years of war and insecurity, the market remains largely informal and national level production is limited. There are few business role models and fewer women-owned businesses. Zardozi's 'pull' strategies, therefore, focus on making introductions and building relationships with informal traders and shopkeepers to facilitate orders for their clients. The gender-related barriers that women face in terms of interacting with male staff members, shopkeepers, and business-owners have limited Zardozi's ability to step away and let market linkages take over. Women need ongoing support and confidence building, not only in terms of engaging in paid work, but also in order-management, branding, marketing, and negotiation in an extremely male-dominated environment. As such, Zardozi plays a key role in managing risk for both the women and the private sector buyers.

Despite these challenges, Zardozi is making headway and remains a unique model in the Afghan context. In just three years, they have facilitated opportunities for approximately 6,000 women. Their members have measured an average fourfold increase in income in traditional value chains ranging from US$16 per month (23 per cent of clients) to over $300 per month (the most entrepreneurial 14 per cent). For example, some women have expanded into new and lucrative markets such as the private school uniform market in Herat where uniforms were purchased previously from Iran. Zardozi helped to identify and connect women to this new market using wholesale fabrics imported from Pakistan. The connection has resulted in the sustained local procurement of uniforms from Zardozi clients with women managing their own orders and relationships with the schools.

The majority of Zardozi's clients (62 per cent) earn between $18 and $62 per month. These women are the most risk averse and focus on raising just enough money to support their family. For the most part, women report being able to reinvest their earnings in their businesses while balancing demands on their income related to children, healthcare, and household expenses. Qualitative surveys also show improvements in women's healthcare and family nutrition; an increase in investments in girls' education; and a new confidence in women to confront gender stereotypes in the communities in which they live. Women mention a change in their status within the family and the community and more agency and control over their incomes. Zardozi's clients have become more mobile as the family sees the benefits of their businesses and that no harm comes to them despite pushing the cultural boundaries of operating in a public space.

Long-term, sustainable economic empowerment for women in Afghanistan will take time and require more effort, and engaging and convincing men and families about the value of women's economic empowerment is critical for Zardozi's clients and for the future of the country. Women's lack of self-confidence and opposition from family members are significant barriers to women's business expansion. Efforts to address this, for example through awareness-raising and celebrations of women's successes, have gone some way to reversing family opposition. Zardozi has found that tackling gender biases through concrete demonstrations of women's economic contributions to their families and communities is an important strategy for building women's social capital in Afghanistan.

ECDI: Entrepreneurship and Community Development Institute in Pakistan

The entrepreneurship and Community development institute (ECDI) has been working for over two decades to support women and the poor to attain their socioeconomic potential. In the past, ECDI focused on building the capacity of individual women entrepreneurs and micro, small, and medium enterprises through training and provision of business development services. However, in recent years, ECDI chose to move from a service provision model to the development of pro-poor markets by stimulating competitiveness among key market players. Value chain analyses showed that social and cultural barriers resulting in women's isolation from the public sphere, prohibited women producers of hand-embellished fabrics from earning fair wages from their labour. ECDI became a key partner in the entrepreneurs project, funded by the United States Agency for international development (2009–2014), which sought to increase women's incomes and access to the high-value hand-embellished fabric market that exists for Pakistani work nationally and abroad.

ECDI's client base for the project was home-bound rural and peri-urban women working on embellished fabrics on a piecework basis. Like Zardozi, ECDI chose to work with women producers and small enterprises as a critical route to increasing women's economic and social capital. In rural Sindh, rural South Punjab, Balochistan, and Swat, hand embellishment is the primary livelihood for women; however, poor women, particularly in rural areas, earn very little and sometimes no return on their labour. Constrained by lack of mobility, violence, ethnic and religious strife, power shortages, and a deteriorating law and order situation, accessing buyers is difficult. Furthermore, home-bound women have limited access to market information, lack quality inputs, and suffer from an absence of credit facilities to improve and expand their production.

ECDI's use of push and pull strategies in Sindh, Pakistan

ECDI was one of the pioneers of an innovative 'push' strategy in Pakistan called the Female Sales Agent model. The model focused on building the capacity and confidence of local women producers, who had a relatively greater degree of mobility within the community, and worked through these Sales Agents to reach other home-bound women. ECDI began with extensive social mobilization of families and communities to create buy-in for women's participation in the project, then identified a cadre of women that could be trained as Sales Agents in business and product marketing. The Female Sales Agents received training in a variety of areas including design, marketing, basic accounting, quality assurance, negotiation skills, and conflict resolution. They also acted as the liaison between the market and other women home-based producers. They brought new product designs, production techniques, and resources to the women; and carried finished products to market; ensuring payment for the home-bound women. Female Sales Agents earned no wages from the project.

The project also set up 15 Common facility Centres (CFC) as hubs for business training and marketing. Unlike Zardozi, the entrepreneur's CFCS were legally registered small businesses operated by a group of women entrepreneurs. Each CFC is now equipped with resource materials, sample catalogues, sample books, training manuals, and other relevant materials. They serve to aggregate women's products and act as informal 'buying houses'. They also have become community centres for the women to meet and work on orders together. As both a 'push' and 'pull' strategy, the CFCS have provided women with important connections to microfinance institutions for loan products and have enabled buyers, marketing, and design teams to interact with large swathes of producers who were previously inaccessible to them. By the close of the project, some CFCs were being supported by private sector companies (such as Asassah, Texlynx, and Indus Heritage Trust) to ensure a continued stream of hand-embellished fabric for their garments.

One 'pull' strategy that ECDI was able to employ has been to help women pitch their handiwork and designs to private sector buyers, thus brokering trust in the market place. Mainstream stores and brands were keen to get into the hand-embroidered product market after seeing the success of home-based boutiques and high-end designers. Through their years of working with women in hand-embellished fabrics, ECDI was able to approach business owners directly with a solid business case. This strategy was well received in Pakistan where the larger companies in the garment and textile sector tend to be male-owned and wary of working with women directly. Connecting private sector actors directly with the women producers built the women's capacity to understand and meet private sector standards around quality and timeliness. ECDI also encouraged the private sector to create incentives versus penalties to help women improve their products and was successful in negotiating bonuses for women who delivered quality products on time.

Under the entrepreneur's project, ECDI helped to create self-employment opportunities for 7,000 women embellishers and 120 Female Sales Agents.

Across the entire project (a total of four value chains), women reported an average increase of 93 per cent in net sales and a 19 per cent average increase in project-related income from 7 per cent to 26 per cent at the household level from 2010 to 2014 (Innovative Development Strategies, 2014). In addition, an independent assessment by Innovative Development Strategies showed that project participants experienced better overall enterprise management with the greatest increase in marketing skills (35 per cent), preservation of outputs (31 per cent), quality control (28 per cent), and linkages to domestic producers (26 per cent). Focus group discussions pointed to a positive change in community attitudes toward women and women's entrepreneurship and a self-reported change in women's status within the household including greater decision-making power, confidence, and independence.

ECDI have continued to help their clients secure contracts and have facilitated linkages between their clients and 17 high-end designer labels in Pakistan and exports to Canada, Italy, and England. They have found that moving into larger and more sophisticated orders will require more oversight from them, a trend that will likely continue given the literacy and confidence challenges facing their women clients. And while some of the educated Female Sales Agents have started using social media and SMS to connect with the market directly, the majority of ECDI's clients continue to remain worlds apart from the growing middle class market in Pakistan that they serve.

MEDA: Mennonite Economic Development Associates in northern Ghana

Mennonite Economic Development Associates (MEDA) has been working for over 60 years to facilitate business solutions to poverty. Statistical data for Ghana shows that women account for approximately 50 per cent of the agricultural labour force and produce around 70 per cent of Ghana's food crops (Ghana Ministry of Food and Agriculture, 2004). Many farmers in northern Ghana are poor. They often own less than 2 acres of land and struggle to produce enough crop in a single rainy season to feed their families for the year. In particular, women farmers are frequently overlooked and under-served. Women have limited knowledge of market players; do not receive technical training from extension agents; and tend to sell produce in small quantities in informal local markets. They are last in line for land preparation services, have limited access to labour-saving technologies and rarely access loans to cover production costs.

However, across the north of the country, women play a significant role in the provision of food and nutrition within families. Although access to land is controlled by men and men control cash crops, women cultivate kitchen gardens and often small plots of marginal land for additional food crops. Surplus produce often is sold to the local market to generate income which is reinvested back in to the household.

In 2012, MEDA undertook a gender and market analysis of the soybean sector in Ghana as part of the design of the Greater Rural Opportunities

(GROW) Project, funded by the Department of Foreign Affairs, Trade and Development Canada (2012–18). The analysis showed that soybean has strong potential as a revenue-generating crop for women in the north and that it could contribute significantly to household diets due to its high nutritional content. The GROW project seeks to work with women soybean farmers to strengthen production and market linkages, increase access to appropriate financial services, and support women farmers to expand the production of nutrition foods and increase nutritional awareness.

MEDA's use of push-pull strategies in Ghana

MEDA adapted a number of successful 'push' strategies to help increase the productivity and profits of women soybean farmers. They began by bringing communities together to talk about gender equality and the roles women and men have been assigned at work and at home. Men and traditional leaders were asked to endorse women's participation in the project and encouraged to think about how they could support the women in their family to be successful farmers, for example through the provision of land to the women. MEDA has found that the identification of male champions, particularly husbands and chiefs that control productive resources in rural communities, is an important strategy for facilitating women's economic empowerment in Ghana.

MEDA also adapted the successful Female Sales Agent model from Pakistan to the GROW project creating a cohort of Women Lead Farmers to train, mentor, and guide other women farmers in their communities in soybean production. The nucleus farmer model, currently promoted in northern Ghana, creates Nucleus Farmers with land holdings of 5–50 acres (predominately men) and provides them with tools to disseminate inputs, services, financing, and product aggregation to hundreds or a thousand farmers. By contrast, the GROW project's Women Lead Farmers are trained as entrepreneurs to provide products and services to 20–30 other women smallholder farmers in their own communities. After basic training in improved agronomic practices, business, and negotiation skills, the lead farmers provide direct extension services, support, and assistance to women in their groups. Like Zardozi and ECDI, MEDA actively connects Women Lead Farmers directly to market actors such as financial service providers, input suppliers, tractor operators, threshing machine service providers, and soybean buyers to facilitate linkages to help 'pull' women's products into market. Through field visits, the women learn about soybean demand, quality, pricing, and market behaviour. They also work within their groups to expand dry season economic activities where market opportunities exist.

In the first three years of the project, MEDA has seen the Women Lead Farmers take on new and different market roles, becoming active agents of change in the market system. Women have become distributors of inputs and extension services to other farmers (male and female) as well as soybean aggregators. The project is supporting some women to become soybean processors, producing value-added products such as soy-milk and tofu to sell in the local retail market. in addition, the project is piloting initiatives with government, private sector businesses, and NGOS to test the efficacy of using the Lead Farmers to disseminate timely market information using information communications technology (e.g. SMS and voicemail messages) and extension advice in local dialects to illiterate farmers through mechanisms such as 'Talking Books'. The talking book, an innovative low-cost audio computer, was designed by literacy bridge and is being piloted through the MedA GROW project.

One difference in MEDA's experience was the way in which MEDA consciously worked on identifying potential 'pull' strategies early in the design of the project to leverage commercial/market actors to help overcome the barriers that face women farmers in the north. At the outset of the project, MedA pitched the business case for working with women to a range of input suppliers, service providers, financial institutions, and soybean processors, encouraging them to tap into the vast new network of women farmers that the project would create as new customers, suppliers, and producers.

MEDA also brought several large soy processing companies to meet the women farmers prior to the first harvest. After seeing the volume of soybeans that were being produced by the women, two companies approached MEDA to negotiate purchases with the women farmers directly. Women's groups were able to secure a competitive market price for their harvested beans and a commitment from the buyers to cover the costs of collection and transport to processing plants in the south. Through this process, community members learned about the value of the women's crop; became energized by the bargaining and competition between firms for their beans; and learned more about how processing companies viewed the women as a key production source to meet Ghana's large unmet soybean demand.

Another 'pull' strategy that the GROW project used was to work with a financial institution to help women farmers access production loans. Sissala Rural Bank lacked the capital to provide small production loans to women farmers so MEDA engineered a three-way partnership arrangement between the bank and a local NGO, whereby MEDA financed a $50,000 loan to the bank which it committed to using for women farmers. The local NGO provided on-the-ground follow-up with the borrowers, facilitated the sales of beans promptly after harvest to ensure repayment and followed-up with any delayed payment. The first year of the project saw a 54 per cent increase in women's access to finance both through voluntary savings and loan associations (VSIAS) and formal loans from sissala bank. The GROW team is now working to help the women form VSIA groups that will invest their savings in agricultural production.

As the project enters its third year, over 11,000 women farmers have been registered, 40 per cent have planted soybeans, and 515 lead farmers are actively working in their communities. The number of women who are producing and selling soybean increased by 44 per cent at the end of the first year, reflecting significantly more connections to processors and other buyers than existed before. Other early impact indicators show that 71 per cent of women reported having access to timely market information, including on such topics as pricing (70 per cent) and potential buyers (20 per cent). Of those female farmers that received market information, 50 per cent of them indicated they were able to negotiate with different buyers to agree on terms of sales such as transportation, pricing, storage, and payments.

Aside from increasing soybean production, women are diversifying their dry-season activities with new crops that will further enhance household income and nutrition. Moving forward, MEDA is devoting resources towards addressing other bottlenecks in the soybean value chain to increase the reach and sustainability of the project. For example, GROW will be working with seed growers to ensure enough available seeds at planting season, linking them to the Women Lead Farmers and Sales Agents, and working with technology suppliers to help improve the availability of hand-held planters to provide more low-cost technology options for women farmers.

MEDA has learned that discussions with private sector actors around the business case for working with women helps market actors view women farmers as clients or suppliers in their own right. Once the case is made, women have a much easier time integrating into the market and the potential for sustainability increases. Christian bellow, Operations Manager for Golden Web Soybean Processing Company said, 'Next year we don't need MEDA to be there. We can buy directly from the women. It is self-sustaining. That's what we are looking for.'

Conclusions

In the authors' experience, the key to designing inclusive market systems development programming lies first in understanding the complexities of the programming environment from a gender, social, and market systems perspective. Each of the three organizations set out to design women's economic empowerment projects that directly addressed the gender discrimination and market challenges that women faced and did so in a way that was culturally sensitive and appropriate. The starting point was to demonstrate to women and their families that they could expand their informal, home-based work as a business; and then to develop the business case for other market actors to help them succeed.

Using a combination of 'push' and 'pull' strategies is critical, particularly when working with poor and marginalized women. 'Push' strategies will help to 'level the playing field', increase women's skills and confidence, and expand women's understanding of the market systems in which they work. All three organizations created networks and spaces for women to connect – for social support, learning, consciousness-raising, and negotiating. Zardozi's Community Business Centres and ECDI's Common Facility Centres provided culturally acceptable, women-only spaces for the project to offer business services and support to more women than could be reached in their individual homes. ECDI's female sales Agent model in Pakistan and MEDA's Women Lead

Farmers model in Ghana are further adaptations that have expanded the reach and scale of women's networks through empowering women in their own communities to assume positions as teachers, leaders, role models, negotiators, and agents of change. It is worth noting that the Female Sales Agents and Lead Farmers are not remunerated by the projects. The women earn income from market-based sales of their products alongside the women in their groups. As such, this innovative model is replicable, scalable, and also sustainable.

'Pull' strategies that bring recognition of women's role in the value chain and market system are easier to employ in countries like Ghana where social and cultural norms and customs are less prohibitive of direct interactions between women and men. However, in all of the case studies, there was some degree of 'pull' (see Figure 9.1). Whether this was facilitating introductions for women garment makers to new markets in Afghanistan or facilitating discussions around design, quality, and timeliness of delivery with buyers and women embroiders in Pakistan, the connections created a spark of awareness about the potential market that existed and the role of women within it. In Ghana, 'pull' strategies such as facilitating women's access to formal credit and demonstrating the business case for engaging women as input suppliers and seed processors in their own communities are examples of how 'pull' can be used to expand private sector reach and women's roles in market systems. As demonstrated by the case studies above, 'push' and 'pull' strategies can increase women's economic empowerment and generate dynamic shifts in gender relations and market systems. They also create potential for lasting change.

Making markets work for women is not easy. For many, facilitation, in market systems development terms, is new. NGOs struggle to catalyse change within market systems without becoming part of the system itself. Continual capacity building within organizations is key but, ultimately, experience is the most effective teacher. No two communities will be the same and adapting and employing successful models will garner new learning. And as Zardozi,

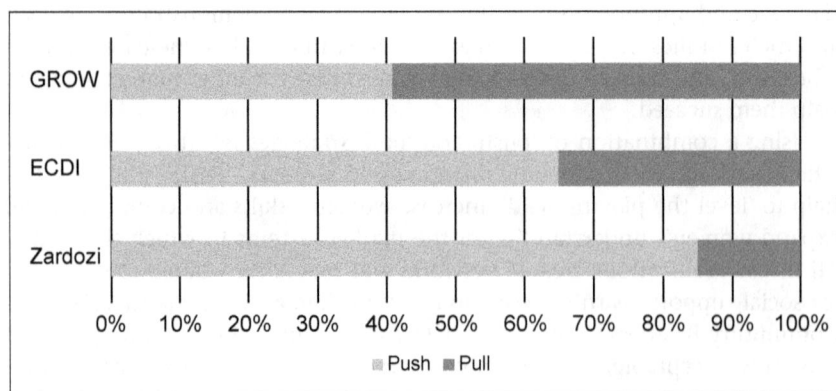

Figure 9.1 Comparison of case studies using push-pull approaches with women

ECDI, and MEDA have learned, celebrating women's successes is key. When community members see buyers that are eager to do business directly with women, they begin to internalize the importance of women's economic empowerment and the transformative potential that it can bring.

About the authors

Christine Faveri (cfaveri@meda.org) is Director, Women's Economic Opportunities at Mennonite Economic Development Associates, Canada; **Kerry Jane Wilson** (wilsonkerryjane@gmail.com) is Director, Zardozi – Markets for Afghan Women at Zardozi, Afghanistan; **Perveen Shaikh** (ecdi_pak@yahoo.com) is President, Entrepreneurship and Community Development Institute, Pakistan.

References

De Santos, A. (2013) *Women's Entrepreneurship Diagnostic*, Washington, DC: USAID.

Ghana Ministry of Food and Agriculture (2004) *Gender and Agricultural Development Strategy*, Accra, Ghana: Ministry of Food and Agriculture.

Goldman Sachs and JBWere Investment Research (2009) *Australia's Hidden Resource: The Economic Case for Increasing Female Participation*, Sydney, Australia: Goldman Sachs and JBWere Investment Research.

Golla, A., Malhotra, A., Nanda, P., and Mehra, R. (2011) *Understanding and Measuring Women's Economic Empowerment: Definition, Framework and Indicators*, Washington, DC: International Centre for Research on Women.

Innovative Development Strategies (Pvt.) Ltd (2014) *Performance Evaluation Impact Assessment: Pakistan Entrepreneurs Project* [online], Islamabad, Pakistan, May 2014 <www.meda.org/impactassessment-report/file> [accessed 1 February 2015].

Jones, L. (2012) *Discussion Paper for an M4P WEE Framework: How can the Making Markets Work for the Poor Framework work for poor women and for poor men?* Durham, UK: Springfield Centre.

Kabeer, N., Mahmud, S., and Tasneem, S. (2011) *Does Paid Work Provide a Pathway to Women's Empowerment? Empirical Findings from Bangladesh*, IDS Working Paper 375, Brighton, UK: Institute of Development studies.

Markel, E., and Jones, L. (2014) *Women's Economic Empowerment: Pushing the Frontiers of Inclusive Market Development* [pdf] <https://www.microlinks.org/sites/default/files/resource/ files/WEE_in_Market_Systems_Framework_final.pdf> [accessed 27 January 2015].

SEEP network (2014) 'USAID calls for practitioner learning from push/pull and inclusive market development' [blog] <www.seepnetwork.org/blog/LEO-call-project-examples-inclusivemarket-development-2> [accessed 27 January 2015].

CHAPTER 10

Whose vision counts? The formulation of vision in community forest enterprises

Hiroyuki Tanaka

Abstract

How do external factors such as donor interventions and government policies influence the competitiveness of community forest enterprises (CFEs)? The author conducted a qualitative study on two second-tier CFEs in Mexico and Guatemala. The study consisted primarily of semi-structured interviews with 125 informants, including CFE personnel, buyers, government institutions, and NGOs. It analysed the influence of the CFE's objectives and establishment process over the corporate culture, and the relationship between second-tier CFEs and affiliated CFEs. The study revealed the importance of the autonomous formulation of corporate vision. External interventions should be based on the producers' agency rather than on the donors' agendas. The vision of an enterprise should be guided by buyers' values. A shift from a 'farmer first' to a 'customer first' culture is of paramount importance for support institutions as well.

Keywords: community forest enterprises, Guatemala, Mexico, competitiveness, policy

Community forest enterprises (CFEs) hold significant importance, not only for forest conservation, but also for local economic development, especially for the livelihoods of forest-dependent people. Much of the literature emphasizes the importance of poverty alleviation through the commercialization of forest products (Lecup and Nicholson, 2000; Arnold, 2002; Mayers and Vermeulen, 2002; Donovan et al., 2006; Farrington and Mitchell, 2006). The economic record of CFEs has, however, been mixed (Molnar et al., 2007; Stoian et al., 2009).

The promotion of small- and medium-scale enterprises, including CFEs, is a topic of debate among donors and development practitioners. Various conceptual frameworks and approaches are applied in development interventions. These include 'value-chain' approaches (Kaplinsky and Morris, 2000; GTZ, 2007), 'supply-chain management' (Handfield and Nicholls, 2002; GTZ, 2007), 'cluster' development (Porter, 1998; Schmitz and Nadvi, 1999), 'business development services' promotion (Harper and Tanburn, 2005), and the 'making markets work for the poor' approach (DFID, 2005; Miehlbradt et al., 2005).

http://dx.doi.org/10.3362/9781780448879.010

Although some of the literature addresses the issue of impact assessment and analyses the impact of value chain intervention by donors (USAID, 2006; Humphrey and Navas-Alemán, 2010; Seville et al., 2011), it is insufficient. In particular, studies are lacking regarding the ways in which external interventions influence corporate policy and the vision of community enterprises.

The study's necessity and purpose

The author conducted a study on how CFEs strengthen their market competitiveness strategies through two second-tier CFEs: Integradora Comunal Forestal de Oaxaca S.A. de C.V. (ICOFOSA) in Oaxaca, Mexico, and Empresa Comunitaria de Servicios del Bosque S.A. (FORESCOM) in Peten, Guatemala. For the purpose of this study, the author defines a second-tier CFE as 'an enterprise which is directly or indirectly (for example, through capital investment) governed by a group of CFEs for the purpose of promoting their business'. Given the exploratory nature of this study and its emphasis on theory building, these cases have been purposefully selected. Mexico and Guatemala are in the vanguard in terms of CFE development in the timber business. Second-tier community enterprises in the forest sector are still rare in the tropics, and these two cases are among the few global benchmark initiatives.

ICOFOSA was established by indigenous forest communities in 2006. Three CFEs producing furniture joined to launch a retail business under the brand 'TIPMUEBLES'. ICOFOSA managed two stores in the City of Oaxaca at the time of the field study. FORESCOM was established in San Benito in 2004 as an umbrella organization of nine CFEs with the aim of providing services related to forest-management consultancy, timber brokering, wood drying, wood processing, and machinery rental services. The field study, conducted from October 2009 to August 2010, consisted primarily of semi-structured interviews with 125 informants from within and outside of the value chain. The author interviewed executives and key personnel of ICOFOSA and FORESCOM and members of the 14 first-tier CFEs: Pueblo Mancomunados, Ixtlán de Juárez, Santiago Textitlán (Oaxaca), AFISAP, Cruce a la Colorada, Árbol Verde, Uaxactún, CUSTOSEL, El Esfuerzo, Impulsores Suchitecos, Laborantes del Bosque, Carmelita, Unión Maya Itza, and La Técnica (Peten).The informants also include buyers, government officials, and service providers such as NGOs. These informants were identified through snowball sampling.

This study was conducted for a PhD dissertation and aims to examine the competitiveness of CFEs from three angles: 1) socio-economic aspects; 2) policy aspects; and 3) business aspects. This paper solely discusses 2) policy aspects. It responds to an overarching question that emerged during the study: 'Whose vision counts in the formulation of the vision of the community enterprise?' The chapter is organized according to the following research questions:

- How did the CFEs' goals and processes of establishment affect the corporate culture and the relationship between second-tier CFEs and affiliated CFEs?

- How have the procurement policies of state institutions and donor interventions influenced the policy and strategies of the CFEs under investigation?

The purpose and process of emergence of CFEs, and their influence on corporate culture

ICOFOSA

ICOFOSA was founded by three indigenous communities whose first-tier CFEs share relatively similar characteristics in terms of maturity and business objectives. For more than two decades, all three CFEs have managed their own natural pine forest totalling 72,841 hectares and operated logging and sawmilling businesses. They have created more than 1,000 direct and indirect positions. The three CFEs separately began producing furniture around the year 2005. Their initial products were purchased in large part by the State Institute of Public Education (IEEPO). They took advantage of the state governor's new policy regarding governmental procurement of certified furniture. The gradually diminishing lots assigned to the three CFEs, however, combined with delayed payment by IEEPO triggered by a civil strike in Oaxaca in 2006, prompted the three CFEs' managers to search for new markets and distribution channels for their furniture. As part of this search, they requested quotes from several department stores for their products. These buyers' low offers disappointed them. Ultimately, they decided to jointly launch their own retail business with kitchen, living room, bedroom, and office furniture. They opened the first branch of TIPMUEBLES in Oaxaca in the same year without any external funding.

From the beginning, ICOFOSA has had clear objectives that the three CFEs shared: 1) to learn about the retail furniture business and to experiment with new lines by taking advantage of direct feedback from the customers; 2) to win large institutional contracts by taking advantage of the highly consolidated production capacity of the three factories; 3) to discover new markets not accessible to the individual CFEs; and 4) to demonstrate their community development initiative to the general public and to attract external support.

The costs of administering TIPMUEBLES stores, including both salaries and rent, are equally borne by the three CFEs regardless of the sales level of each factory. ICOFOSA is firmly controlled by the three CFEs as their own 'instrument'. This arrangement protects the corporate policy and vision from external intervention, ICOFOSA is not strictly required to be self-sufficient and any deficits are covered by the three CFEs. This dependency weakens ICOFOSA's autonomy regarding product design and customer service. Instead of the stores directing the factories as to what products to produce, the factories decide what products to sell in the stores. This arrangement differs from private business, where retailers as buyers dictate instructions to the producers. It has delayed the establishment of a unified TIPMUEBLES product style.

Nevertheless, the quality of the products and customer service has significantly improved thanks to direct interaction with customers.

Although the three CFEs are not yet satisfied with ICOFOSA's profit margin, all of them consider it to be part of their long-range strategy for broader diversification. Each CFE individually has parallel sales efforts with other retailers. ICOFOSA respects the autonomy of the first-tier CFEs and does not intervene in the arrangements between them and their existing buyers. Instead, it has attempted to identify new markets at the national level, for example, by participating in furniture expos. The three CFEs also appreciate ICOFOSA's function of winning new governmental contracts. The contracts guarantee institutional buyers timely delivery based on the firm's highly consolidated production capacity.

The CFEs also value ICOFOSA's 'showcase' function. The initiative is branded as a key component of the 'Oaxacan community-based green economy'. As such, it attracts significant assistance from various government institutions as well as NGOs, including financial assistance for expanding the exhibit space in one store and for participating in furniture expos. It has also attracted technical assistance to improve interior installations in both stores.

FORESCOM

FORESCOM was founded as a spin-off venture of the Community Forestry Association of Peten (ACOFOP), with considerable financial assistance from a donor. It was positioned as part of the phase-out strategy of a donor project. The project formerly funded forest management consultancies for CFEs once provided by local NGOs. The donor led the process of formulation. The project aimed to quickly form an organization at the second-tier level and succeeded in convincing the leaders of nine CFEs. The initiative was not well rooted in each CFE's individual strategy, however, thereby limiting the effectiveness of follow-up processes. There was limited information sharing among the CFEs. Owing to the hasty process, true 'buy-in' among members of each CFE was not secured.

The maturity and geographic distribution of the affiliated CFEs was heterogeneous. Some already had their own sawmill, while others sold standing trees. Some CFEs in the Usmacinta region are located far from San Benito, where FORESCOM is located. Even those leaders who were convinced of the project's value were uncertain as to its final form. They had unfocused expectations regarding such aspects as group negotiation with buyers for better prices, international commercial liaisons, value addition, forest-management consultancy, and group certification. Rather than prioritize the services, however, FORESCOM attempted to pursue every service at once. Coordination among the donors and local NGOs was insufficient. The establishment of FORESCOM initially caused friction with the local NGOs because the forest-management consultancy service once provided by local NGOs with donor funding was taken over by FORESCOM.

Various donors and other financial agencies came and left. They did not work for long-term success, but rather changed personnel and priorities. They consequently shifted the focus of FORESCOM's activities from time to time. The original aim of establishing a second-tier enterprise was to create a self-sustaining body of forest-management consultancy services so that the termination of the project would not cause a technical problem for the first-tier CFEs. The interest of one donor in preventing forest fires also triggered the establishment of the Department of Machinery. Other donors suggested incorporating the commercialization of forest products. These various initiatives were not necessarily prompted by the shared interests of affiliated CFEs.

The commercialization of forest products was experimentally handled by the Trade Liaison Office of ACOFOP before the establishment of FORESCOM. This initiative had a significant amount of success. In that period, one single buyer paid seven different prices to communities, taking advantage of weak information-sharing among them. Four CFEs then consolidated their individually produced wood for group negotiation. They managed to sell mahogany for US$1,144/m³, while the other CFEs that negotiated individually were only able to obtain a price of $890/m³ (Hidalgo and Pasos, 2008). Due to legal constraints of ACOFOP as a civil association, however, the function was eventually transferred to FORESCOM, whose legal status as a private company allows for commercial activities. It initially succeeded in obtaining a unified price with a 1 per cent price increase and an interest-free advance payment from two US buyers in 2004 (Hidalgo and Pasos, 2008). The price of mahogany steadily increased because of the low price originally depressed by buyers and its scarcity in the market until the global economic crisis in 2008. Group negotiations organized under FORESCOM may have prompted this price increase.

FORESCOM has met expectations for lower fees for forest management consultancy and group certification. With respect to timber processing, the quality of products has increased, as evidenced by the increased number of buyers at the national level. Despite initial successes, however, progress in the area of timber commercialization has been disappointing. Opinions among affiliated CFEs confirm this conclusion. FORESCOM's marketing efforts have generally been passive. Its capacity to uncover markets remains no better than that of individual member CFEs. What FORESCOM does have is well-developed small-market niches. The prices offered by FORESCOM were no better than those offered by the existing buyers. It hardly made sense to centralize timber sales if FORESCOM could not locate a new market that could provide a higher price for a consolidated volume.

Clear roles are also not established between FORESCOM and the affiliated CFEs. The CFEs are often reluctant to provide timber that meets FORESCOM's specifications. Instead, the CFEs prefer to sell timber to a buyer who purchases all of the lots, regardless of dimensions and quality. Even after FORESCOM negotiated agreements, some CFEs cancelled the sales upon finding a better-paying buyer. This act led to a breach of contracts and cancellations of sales between FORESCOM and external buyers. FORESCOM then meddled in deals between first-tier CFEs and their existing buyers. FORESCOM asked CFEs to sell timber to them out of moral obligation. Some CFEs preferred direct selling to their existing buyers and stopped dealing with FORESCOM altogether.

Different funding agencies provided assistance and investment inducement in different areas, including a seed fund for the commercialization of lesser-known species (LKSs), the purchase of woodworking machinery, the establishment of the Department of Machinery, and the construction of timber-drying kilns. These investments were often justified by an optimistic notion of value addition, despite concerns expressed by affiliated CFEs. Development interventions have an intrinsic risk of the 'Abilene paradox': the assistance recipients may be unconsciously led during the 'participatory' process to say what the facilitator or consultant wants to hear, concealing their misgivings and minimizing the importance of their doubts (Cooke, 2001). Some of the investments were of an experimental and high-risk nature. They have often been guided by donor-funded consultancies as if they were a donor 'project', however, FORESCOM later experienced the consequences as a private enterprise.

Community leaders and the staff of technical support institutions have attended a number of trade fairs. They concluded that CFEs needed to begin processing semi-finished wall and flooring products, taking advantage of the abundance of LKSs such as *Santa María (Callophyllum brasiliense), manchiche (Lonchocarpus castilloi)*, and *pucté (Bucida buceras)* in concession areas. FORESCOM once attempted a partnership with local private industries for processing hardwood species. The partner did not fulfil expectations because of chronic weaknesses, such as the poor maintenance of equipment. The decision-makers assumed that FORESCOM should make investments in machinery themselves and achieve full ownership of the forestry supply chain in Peten (Hidalgo and Pasos, 2008). The first-tier CFEs have in reality demonstrated limited interest in strengthening the commercialization of LKSs. Their high-cost production structure, subsidized by sales of mahogany *(Swietenia macrophylla)*, had not allowed them to enter the market. Many interviewed buyers of LKSs noted that they were treated as second-class buyers by the first-tier CFEs. The majority of the CFEs only pay attention to the customers of mahogany. Some more advanced CFEs are willing to add value to lower-grade mahogany through the production of furniture or doors or to promote eco-tourism and other non-timber forest products such as *xate (Chamaedorea* spp.) over LKSs.

There was little to gain in making a concerted effort at the second-tier level when the first-tier CFEs made a limited effort. Despite strong interest among some donors and the provision of seed funding and technical assistance in processing and the maintenance of equipment, FORESCOM's actions in sales of LKSs were limited to a series of what might best be described as 'spot trading'. They did not make a strategic effort to ask the affiliated CFEs to provide firm-specific information, such as inventory information, to consolidate their fluctuating inventories. This kind of effort is crucial for brokering binding agreements between first-tier CFEs and buyers. Buyers require a steady supply of a certain volume of timber to develop markets in foreign countries such as Vietnam and China. The harvest of LKSs did not significantly increase after months-long capacity-building courses on processing LKSs offered to sawmill operators from 10 CFEs. FORESCOM did not follow up with commercial liaison efforts.

Once the seed funding for commercializing LKSs disappeared, FORESCOM suffered from chronic shortages of working capital. Facing this situation, FORESCOM invested in two additional wood-kilns under the inducement of consultancies provided by an international non-profit financial institution almost immediately after the construction of the first kiln, donated by the Ministry of Agriculture, Livestock and Food (MAGA). Unfortunately, they did not make a staged investment so that they could begin on a small scale and monitor the growth of demand. Currently, the kilns are severely under-utilized because many international buyers have their own kilns. It is also inconvenient to use a kiln for an individual CFE because the required volume to operate it is too large.

After FORESCOM fell into debt for two kilns, it diverted the buyers' funds for the timber consigned by first-tier CFEs to pay the administrative costs. FORESCOM consequently failed to make its payments to the first-tier CFEs. Weak control of the contracts also worsened the matter. The relationship between them deteriorated. It is ironic that first-tier CFEs currently assist FORESCOM with services because of a moral or political commitment.

The establishment of the Department of Machinery is another example of haphazard intervention. The decision to purchase machinery was made under heavy donor influence. The original intention was to purchase machinery to control forest fires. It was difficult, however, to purchase forestry machinery such as tractors for opening firebreaks, because of environmental regulations. The machinery purchased (that is graders, compacting rollers, and excavators) was not logging equipment, which the affiliated CFEs needed. The donor wanted to purchase them partly because the logging equipment was restricted by the environmental regulations and partly because it can only be operated during the harvest season. The new Department of Machinery had little to do with forestry operation or fire control. Nevertheless, its actions were justified by their expected function of generating supplemental revenue for the administration of the enterprise. The CFEs eventually accepted the premise so as not to lose the donation. The revenue raised by the department has primarily been utilized to cover the enterprise's administrative costs.

This donor's intervention eventually placed the profitability of the enterprise in jeopardy. Reinvestment in new machinery for offering a new service has been limited because of the department's marginal position in the enterprise. Many of the clients have already obtained similar types of machinery and no longer require the services once provided by the department. The recent global financial crisis has also reduced the public works budget. The department has found it difficult to recover from the dramatic reduction of sales.

The inconsistency in corporate vision is closely related to weak corporate governance. The strategies and monitoring have been inconsistently administered because of the frequent rotation of managers. Neither did donors offer sufficient capacity-building in enterprise administration in parallel. Little buy-in towards FORESCOM among ordinary members of first-tier CFEs weakened the board members' position. Community leaders did not understand the necessity of hiring a well-compensated, professional manager. The limited professionalism among the board members caused role confusion with the management of FORESCOM. At times, the board members intervened in the firm's administration in an inappropriate manner. There was even a period when the manager could not sign cheques, whereas the president of the board and the treasurer could. The lack of a remuneration system linked with actual performance has inflated the costs of personnel. It also hindered effective management control by the board. It affected the managers' accountability towards the affiliated CFEs. Some members of the affiliated CFEs regret that FORESCOM's financial reports were prepared more for the donors, while the affiliated CFEs themselves were not informed about FORESCOM's deficit.

This situation has cultivated an ambiguity regarding responsibility. Neither politically appointed *campesino* (country folk) managers – a criticism used by some buyers – or externally recruited professional managers with short-term moral commitment have taken responsibility for the enterprise's financial performance.

Influence of government procurement policy and donor interventions on the vision of CFEs

A fundamental difference between the two cases lies in the quality of external influence in the development of corporate vision. The Oaxacan government's procurement of certified furniture – along with the CFEs' own spontaneous efforts to learn product design, quality control, store presentation, publicity, and customer relations at ICOFOSA – has contributed to creating a customer-oriented culture among the concerned CFEs.

Unfortunately, a donor-led foundation meddled in FORESCOM's goals and vision from the beginning. Many donors came and went. It is hardly possible to differentiate the influence of an enterprise's emergence process on corporate culture from the influence of donor interventions because the enterprise's history so closely parallels the history of donor interventions. By whose agency the enterprise is actually driven has been blurred. Without clear role definition between the second-tier and the first-tier actors, the enterprise's policy and vision remain adrift while the firm continues to rely on external assistance.

Influence of the government's furniture procurement policy

The Oaxacan state policy regulating the acquisition of certified furniture for government institutions has exerted a significant influence over the launching of furniture production among the three CFEs. IEEPO has supported this community-based industry since its foundation, placing a series of orders valued at 116 million pesos (US$1 = 12.63 Mexican pesos on 13 March 2012) between 2006 and 2009.

This policy has effectively aligned with the three CFEs' learning process. It has stimulated improvement on the part of the producers. IEEPO requests annual design modifications that convey the preference of final users for lighter, stronger, and more comfortable furniture. The three CFEs jointly submit counterproposals that meet IEEPO requirements while minimizing the production costs by adapting 'design for production' (Herrmann, 2003). IEEPO also provides a contract to associations of local carpenters, and penalizes those who cannot meet the scheduled delivery date by diminishing the volume of the contract in the following year. IEEPO has a clear sense of its role as a catalyst for community-based initiatives and sustains this responsibility in the form of long-term commitments.

At the same time, IEEPO forces the producers to compete with one another. They are gradually diminishing the total volume of their orders each year to induce the producers to diversify their market. In other words, they provide a grace period for community-based industries to mature and become self-sufficient. The three CFEs are expanding the sales to other government institutions to compensate for the reduction in the IEEPO orders while developing a strategy to strengthen the sales through TIPMUEBLES and other distribution channels.

Influence of donor interventions

Lusby (2006) argues that external interventions should avoid being overly prescriptive or heavy-handed in determining what the structure of the market relationship should be or what activities to engage in. Claus Offe (quoted in Doner and Schneider, 2000: 270) indicates that organizations of firms 'do not generate power that does not already exist, nor do they formulate ends that do not derive directly from the ends already defined and consciously pursued at the level of the individual member firms'.

There is a striking difference between ICOFOSA and FORESCOM in this respect. The former has received significant external assistance from various institutions, however, its corporate policy or vision does not oscillate. The organization exercises its agency to make its own decisions. It only takes risks that the organization can bear. Once the organization makes a decision, it is willing to suffer the consequences. Furniture retail conducted at ICOFOSA derives from the concrete corporate strategies of each affiliated CFE, regardless of the external assistance that it sometimes receives.

Unfortunately, external assistance often directs the investment policy of the recipient, as the FORESCOM case indicates. Donors intervene in formulating corporate vision, which should be autonomous. There is a tendency among donors and NGOs to be less demand driven. They are prone to becoming internally focused and convinced that they are doing the right thing (see Drucker, 1990). They often do not understand the appropriate balance of risks and returns expected by the buyers, in part because they lack 'business DNA' (Hoffman, 2005) and in part because they themselves do not assume any risk in case of failure. The adherence of FORESCOM's donors to the notion of value addition is an indicative example. Their 'cause marketing' may ultimately become 'cause selling': instead of learning customers' circumstances, they push the sellers' concepts. They believe that they have a good product and do not attempt to understand why people are not rushing to purchase it (Kotler interviewed by Drucker, 1990). The products and services of donor-assisted CFEs at times reflect more of what the donors believe is appropriate rather than what the market demands (see Lusby, 2006). What represents 'value' to the producer is not necessarily in accordance with the final customer or the intermediary who makes the buying decision. Adding value can be treacherous if it is not implemented carefully (Clay, 1997). Buyers do not demand timber certification in the same way that forest authorities, donors, and NGOs do. The CFEs tend to charge what represents 'costs', while the buyers are only willing to pay for value. 'Businesses are not paid to reform customers. They are paid to satisfy customers' (Drucker, 1985: 193). An external FORESCOM buyer who respects its philosophy still criticizes it for its 'socialist business model', which is not acceptable to the buyers.

Lusby (2006) argues that many external interventions are group-focused. They first establish a group and provide capacity-building assistance, and then they look for a market. They tend to try to go around 'exploitative' intermediaries and sell directly to large-scale buyers or to alternative fairtrade markets (Miehlbradt et al., 2005;Lusby, 2006). They may shift trade 'to flow through farmer cooperatives as the intermediary of choice' (Seville et al., 2011: 44). Their understanding of the role of intermediaries is often inadequate. They tend to underestimate the required capacity and costs of bypassing the intermediaries. Intermediaries often offer very important embedded services, for example, many CFEs in Peten appreciate a local intermediary's commercial liaison function. He searches for different buyers in different countries on behalf of the producers, so that the various grades of timber can be marketed effectively.

A new initiative must be built on what already exists, rather than supplanting the old with newly imported models in order to be both sustainable and locally owned (Committee of Donor Agencies for Small Enterprise Development, 2001; Seville et al., 2011). Instead of attempting to eliminate intermediaries, it is critically important to understand who the existing market players are and what function they serve to address 'systemic constraints' and to explore how to work with both intermediaries and producers to reduce the inefficiencies that cause high costs or low prices. Only market actors understand what is feasible or not from their own perspectives. It is always preferable to engage the targeted market players, such as producers, traders, wholesalers, and transporters in the design of programme interventions (Lusby, 2006). Group negotiations with buyers commonly observed in traditional group approaches tend to aim to strengthen the power of small producers, whereas it also reduces buyers' transaction costs for dealing with many small producers. Addressing systemic constraints at the value-chain level, however, has the potential to 'enlarge the pie', creating a new market with a leverage of reduced costs or added value. It offers benefits not only for small producers but also for other value-chain actors, and thus, it is more likely to be accepted.

Doner and Schneider (2000) argue that the institutional capacity to induce members to commit resources and abide by the collective rules and decisions provides a good indicator of the strength of an association. The satisfaction and buy-in of each member firm is strongly connected with the benefits they receive. Any first-tier CFE's decision regarding collaboration with a second-tier CFE is based on an assessment of the benefits on one hand and the costs and risks on the other. However, 'often, the benefits will be long term and hypothetical, whereas costs and risks are obvious and immediate' (Meyer-Stamer, 2003: 21). In the case of FORESCOM, relatively cheap technical services of forest-management consultancy and group certification have served as the bottom-line benefits prompting the CFEs to remain affiliated with it. They expected FORESCOM to perform as a 'soft' network (Rosenfeld, 1996) for solving common problems such as buyers playing pricing games. They expect a reduction in the 'transaction costs' through loose coordination rather than a reduction in the 'adaptive costs' through active joint investment (see Macqueen, 2004).

In a traditional group approach among small farmers, the less group management that is required, the greater the chance of success. The group may be more effective at simpler functions such as representation and advocacy, information sharing, capacity-building, joint purchase of raw materials, and value-chain coordination (Miehlbradt et al., 2005; Lusby, 2006). The same tendency is often observed in a soft network of small enterprises. It may be unfair to expect a soft network to be a joint venture. Affiliated CFEs, however, did not forcibly control FORESCOM. They did not make an effort or bear the costs so that it could align with their true aspirations. They have consequently let the vision and focus drift because the initiative was not 'theirs' from the beginning. They had little motivation to collaborate because of their diversity in maturity, business strategies, and geographic locations.

Initiatives with heavy donor leverage either intentionally or unintentionally shy away from inconvenient business realities. FORESCOM and support institutions were not serious enough in convincing affiliated CFEs of the strategic importance of cost reduction because of their conflicting support for employment creation and improved welfare. For their part, CFEs indulge themselves with high mahogany prices without a conscious effort. Ironically, the abundance of mahogany itself became a systemic constraint. Crises at times offer opportunities, whereas complacency creates problems (Drucker, 1985).

The CFEs offer their employees higher wages and better social security than do competing private industries. They also provide better food, electricity, and recreational facilities in the work camps. As a social enterprise, it is justifiable for the CFEs to incur such costs. Some CFEs even assign an 'assistant of assistant' who has few responsibilities. Such inefficient operations with inflated payrolls have been tolerated in the name of 'job creation'. In serious cases, community members demanded Christmas bonuses even when the CFE was running at a deficit, urging it to obtain loans from private lenders who charged high interest. Few CFEs dare to face their own disadvantages in terms of high costs, irregular volume, and lack of long-term commitment with buyers, thus limiting their marketing horizon. When 'local firms are increasingly forced to perform to global standards not just in matters of costs but also quality, speed of response, and flexibility' (Schmitz and Nadvi, 1999: 1507), buyers do not see that those CFEs are making a serious effort to satisfy customers. A CFE, which supposedly embraces the cause of CFEs, even chose a private contractor who paid a higher price for their standing trees rather than selling the same trees to a neighbouring CFE. The latter invested in a high-capacity sawmill, assuming that it could also purchase logs from neighbouring communities. The CFE offered a log price 10 per cent lower than that of private competitors, however, because of its high cost structure. The sawmill remains idle for many months each year, despite a high depreciation cost.

Donors' heavy influence also nurtures a culture of dependence and obscures responsibility for the deficit and failed projects. Ostrom (2000) argues that norms set by the community members themselves seem to improve performance and encourage cooperative behaviour over time, whereas externally imposed rules may disappear very quickly. The worst results occur when external authorities impose rules but are only able to achieve weak monitoring and sanctioning. The mild degree of external monitoring discourages the formation of social norms, whereas it makes deceit attractive to some actors who appreciate the low risk of being caught.

The sense of responsibility among the donors has also been blurred. Drifting policy and change of personnel in donor interventions made the CFEs 'a prisoner' in a sense. The phenomenon seems to be partially rooted in the industry's structural problem that 'it pays to be ignorant' (Pritchett, 2002). Meyer notes the general bias in the development industry:

> The evaluator/consultants want another job so they mute their criticisms, the sharp edges of evaluation reports get smoothed over as the draft moves up the chain of command for comment, the practical problems of working in tough environments get emphasized as a way to soften the fact of lack of impact (Meyer, 2006: 22).

Conclusion

The goals and processes of CFEs' establishment exert a decisive influence on the CFEs' corporate culture and vision. The comparison of ICOFOSA and FORESCOM demonstrates the importance of 'producer agency', which has been under-emphasized in value-chain interventions (Seville et al., 2011). The issue is not whether second-tier CFEs can promote the development of

CFEs or not. Rather, what matters most are the vision and agency held by the first-tier CFEs. ICOFOSA has always been under the strategic control of three affiliated CFEs, although it has also received considerable external assistance. As long as the first-tier CFEs commit themselves to using the second-tier CFE as their own instrument, the second-tier CFE will maintain a good potential to function. Otherwise, its chance of success will be slim. A second-tier institution of community enterprises does not command power or drive initiatives that do not derive from the true aspirations of the first-tier enterprises.

IEEPO's commitment as a buyer has strengthened producer agency. It has enacted its environmental and social agenda in a commercially feasible way. IEEPO also effectively utilizes competition among producers as a stimulant for the continuous improvement of product quality and services. The gradual reduction in purchases effectively works as a phase-out strategy, urging CFEs to diversify their markets to function independently.

In contrast, the donor-led foundation 'buttoned up the shirt crookedly' and blurred FORESCOM's corporate vision. It weakened the buy-in among many first-tier CFEs. It is ironic that first-tier CFEs are steadily maturing professionally on their own account. A key international buyer dispatches experts every year for approximately eight years so that the CFEs can meet the quality requirements of the US market. This assistance has significantly contributed to the advancement of concerned CFEs. Six or seven first-tier CFEs in Peten are already deemed quite mature by the buyers in terms of their quality control.

The vision of an enterprise should be guided by buyers' values. Relying upon the intuition or desires of CFE executives does not make sense unless the buyers offer positive feedback. CFEs tend to move in the right direction only when they align their products and services with buyers' demand. Whereas the clients are always the 'kings' of the market, development institutions and practitioners traditionally embrace a 'farmer first' philosophy (Chambers, 1983). Development institutions do not assume the risks and consequences of their interventions, however, a fact that allows them to forward their agenda. Any interventions regarding investment decisions or other strategic moves should be based on producer agency and made in a way that nurtures and strengthens the producer's own agency. External inducements based on a certain ethical consideration or rights-based commitment cannot be more than a secondary element. A shift from a 'farmer first' to a 'customer first' culture is of paramount importance for support institutions as well.

About the authors

Hiroyuki Tanaka (hiroyuki.tanaka@vandals.uidaho.edu) is a Consultant in the International Cooperation Department of Kaihatsu Management Consulting, Inc. The author would like to express sincere appreciation to Dietmar Stoian, Ronnie de Camino (CATIE), Steven Hollenhorst, and Steven Shook (University of Idaho) for their comments and mentoring.

References

Arnold, M. (2002) 'Identifying links between forests and poverty', discussion paper presented at the *ECT/IIED Forestry and Poverty Reduction Workshop*, Edinburgh, UK, 13 June 2002.

Blanchard, D. (2007) *Supply Chain Management: Best Practices*, John Wiley & Sons, Hoboken, NY.

Chambers, R. (1983) *Rural Development: Putting the Last First*, Longman Scientific & Technical, Harlow, UK.

Clay, J.W. (1997) 'Business and biodiversity: Rain forest marketing and beyond', in N.C. Vance and J. Thomas (eds), *Special Forest Products: Biodiversity Meets the Marketplace*, pp. 122–45 [ebook], US Department of Agriculture, Forest Service, Washington, DC <http://www.fs.fed.us/pnw/pubs/gtr63/gtrwo63h.pdf> [accessed 8 October 2010].

Committee of Donor Agencies for Small Enterprise Development (2001) *Business Development Services for Small Enterprises: Guiding Principles for Donor Intervention* [ebook] <http://www.enterprise-development.org/download.aspx?id=1291> [accessed 4 May 2012].

Cooke, B. (2001) 'The social psychological limits of participation?' in B. Cooke and U. Kothari (eds), *Participation: The New Tyranny?* pp. 102–21, Zed Books, London.

Department for International Development (DFID) (2005) 'Making market systems work better for the poor (M4P): An introduction to the concept' [website], discussion paper prepared for the *ADB-DFID 'Learning Event'*, ADB, Manila <http://www.urbanlandmark.org.za/downloads/DFID_M4P_An_introduction_to_the_concept.pdf> [accessed 22 May 2010].

Doner, R. and Schneider, B. (2000) 'Business associations and economic development: Why some associations contribute more than others', *Business and Politics* 2(3): 260–88, http://dx.doi.org/10.2202/1469-3569.1011

Donovan, J., Stoian, D., Macqueen, D. and Grouwels, S. (2006) 'The business side of sustainable forest management: Small and medium forest enterprise development for poverty reduction', in *Natural Resource Perspectives*, 104, Overseas Development Institute, London.

Drucker, P. (1985) *Innovation and Entrepreneurship: Practice and Principles*, HarperCollins, New York.

Drucker, P. (1990) *Managing the Nonprofit Organization: Principles and Practices*, HarperCollins, New York.

Farrington, J. and Mitchell, J. (2006) 'How can the rural poor participate in global economic processes?' in *Natural Resource Perspectives 103* [website], Overseas Development Institute <http://www.odi.org.uk/resources/download/35.pdf> [accessed 5 August 2009].

GTZ (2007) *ValueLinks Manual: The Methodology of Value Chain Analysis* [ebook], GTZ <http://edu.care.org/Documents/GTZ%20ValueLinks%20Manual.pdf> [accessed 8 September 2011].

Handfield, R. and Nicholls, E. (2002) *Supply Chain Redesign: Transforming Supply Chains into Integrated Value Chain Systems*, Financial Times Prentice Hall, Upper Saddle River, NJ.

Harper, M. and Tanburn, J. (eds) (2005) *Mapping the Shift in Business Development Services: Making Markets Work for the Poor*, ITDG Publishing, New Delhi, India.

Herrmann, J.W. (2003) 'Design for production: Concepts and applications', in *Proceedings of the SME East Coast Region 3 Annual Members Conference* [website] <http://www.isr.umd.edu/Labs/CIM/projects/dfp/r3memcon.pdf> [accessed 23 September 2011].

Hidalgo, N.S. and Pasos, R. (2008) 'Lessons from trade in community forest products: Guatemala', in Duncan Macqueen (ed.), *Distinguishing Community Forest Products in the Market: Industrial Demand for a Mechanism that Brings Together Forest Certification and Fair Trade,* Small and Medium Forest Enterprise Series No. 22, pp. 73–88 [ebook], IIED, Edinburgh, UK <http://www.rightsandresources.org/documents/files/doc_579.pdf> [accessed 28 January 2011].

Hoffman, K. (2005) 'Aid Industry Reform and the Role of Enterprise' *Oil, Gas and Energy Law* 3, www.ogel.org/article.asp?key=1934 [accessed 9 May 2012].

Humphrey, J. and Navas-Alemán, L. (2010) *Value Chains, Donor Interventions and Poverty Reduction: A Review of Donor Practice,* IDS Research Report Vol. 2010, No. 63 [ebook], IDS, Brighton, UK <http://www.ids.ac.uk/files/dmfile/rr63.pdf> [accessed 15 September 2011].

Kaplinsky, R. and Morris, M. (2000) *A Handbook for Value Chain Research*, IDRC, Ottawa, Canada.

Lecup, I. and Nicholson, K. (2000) *Community-Based Tree and Forest Product Enterprises: Market Analysis and Development,* FAO, Rome.

Lusby, F. (2006) 'Useful principles for adopting a market development approach for enterprise development organizations', *International Journal of Emerging Markets* 1(4): 341–47<http://dx.doi.org/10.1108/17468800610703388>.

Macqueen, D. (2004) *Associations of Small and Medium Forest Enterprise* [website], IIED, Edinburgh, UK <http://pubs.iied.org/pdfs/13512IIED.pdf> [accessed 9 May 2012].

Mayers, J. and Vermeulen, S. (2002) *Company–Community Forestry Partnerships: From Raw Deals to Mutual Gains? An International Review with Proposals for Improving Forests, Enterprise and Livelihoods,* IIED, London.

Meyer-Stamer, J. (2003) 'Obstacles to cooperation in clusters and how to overcome them', *Developing Alternatives* 9(1): 19–24 <http://www.meyer-stamer.de/2003/JMS-Cluster-DevelopingAlternatives.pdf> [accessed 9 May 2012].

Meyer, R. (2006) 'Re: Day One: Defining impact assessment', in *Impact Assessment: An Online Speaker's Corner Discussion Led by Gary Woller and Hosted by Microlinks.org & USAID,* pp. 22–23 [ebook] <http://microlinks.kdid.org/sites/microlinks/files/resource/files/SC14.pdf> [accessed 11 October 2011].

Miehlbradt, A., McVay, M. and Tamburn, J. (2005) *From BDS to Making Markets Work for the Poor: The 2005 Reader* [ebook]. ILO <http://www.value-chains.org/dyn/bds/docs/452/Reader_2005_final_LOW_RES.pdf> [accessed 8 May 2012].

Molnar, A., Liddle, M., Bracer, C., Khare, A., White, A. and Bull, J. (2007) *Community-Based Forest Enterprises: Their Status and Potential in Tropical Countries* [ebook], ITTO Technical Series #28 <http://www.itto.int/direct/topics/topics_pdf_download/topics_id=37100000&no=1&disp=inline> [accessed 30 October 2011].

Ostrom, E. (2000) 'Collective action and the evolution of social norms', *Journal of Economic Perspectives* 14(3): 137–58, http://dx.doi.org/10.1257/jep.14.3.137.

Porter, M. (1998) 'Cluster and the new economics of competition', *Harvard Business Review*, Nov–Dec 1998: 77–90.

Pritchett, L. (2002) 'It pays to be ignorant: A simple political economy of rigorous program evaluation', *The Journal of Policy Reform* 5(4): 251–69, http://dx.doi.org/10.1080/1384128032000096832

Rosenfeld, S. (1996) 'Does cooperation enhance competitiveness? Assessing the impacts of inter-firm collaboration', *Research Policy* 25: 247–63, http://dx.doi.org/10.1016/0048-7333(95)00835-7.

Schmitz, H. and Nadvi, K. (1999) 'Clustering and industrialization: Introduction', *World Development* 27(9): 1503–14, http://dx.doi.org/10.1016/S0305-750X(99)00072-8.

Seville, D., Buxton, A. and Vorley, B. (2011) *Under What Conditions are Value Chains Effective Tools for Pro-Poor Development?* [website], IIED <http://pubs.iied.org/pdfs/16029IIED.pdf> [accessed 30 October 2011].

Stoian, D., Donovan, J. and Poole, N. (2009) 'Unlocking the development potential of community forest enterprises: Findings from a comparative study in Asia, Africa, Latin America, and the United States' [website], paper presented at the *XIII World Forestry Congress,* Buenos Aires, Argentina, 18–23 October 2009 <http://www.catie.ac.cr/BancoMedios/Documentos%20PDF/development%20potential%20of%20cfe%20-%20stoian%20et%20al%202009.pdf> [accessed 22 November 2010].

USAID (2006) *Impact Assessment: An Online Speaker's Corner Discussion Led by Gary Woller and Hosted by Microlinks.org* [ebook] <http://microlinks.kdid.org/sites/microlinks/files/resource/files/SC14.pdf> [accessed 2 October 2011].

CHAPTER 11

Can the poorest be helped by any of our current models of economic development?

Ben Fowler and Linda Jones

Abstract

Our economic approaches, from graduation approaches to market development, can only do so much to alleviate the deepest poverty. In this debate between two experts, Ben Fowler and Linda Jones argue the case surrounding including the poorest in our models of economic development.

Keywords: graduation models; cash transfers; push–pull models; value chains; microfinance

Linda Jones: I am surprising even myself by taking the stand that the poorest cannot be helped by any of our current models of economic development from graduation approaches to market development. For someone who has worked in value-chain development, M4P, livelihoods, women's economic empowerment, and so on – and seen many success stories – this seems like a strange stand to take. (As a point of clarification, we should stress that the 'current models' referred to here are the common approaches that we use as development practitioners, such as cash transfers, microfinance, enterprise development, and value-chain/market development.)

I have come to believe that our economic approaches can only do so much to alleviate the deepest poverty and that these wins are often short-lived. With brutal land grabs in Africa, the horrendous gender statistics from 'middle income' India, the growing disparity between rich and poor worldwide including developed countries such as our own – what impact are we really having? In countries torn by civil war and ethnic violence, in others where corruption is the modus operandi, and in yet others where women (the poorest of the poor) are mistreated in every conceivable way, what can we achieve that is impactful and sustainable? In 2000, the World Bank published a collection that drew on the 'voices' of more than 60,000 poor women and men from 60 countries (World Bank, 2000). The goal was to understand poverty from the perspective of the poor themselves, and documents the struggles and aspirations of poor people around the world. A key concern of poor people is their lack of access to economic opportunities – this is just the thing that we address in our economic development

http://dx.doi.org/10.3362/9781780448879.011

programmes. Poor people are also acutely aware of their lack of voice, power, and independence, which subjects them to exploitation. The World Bank report notes that this poverty also leaves them vulnerable to rudeness, humiliation, and inhumane treatment by both private and public agents from whom they seek help.

In graduation models, we start by providing a leg-up to people in the deepest poverty, helping them with basic needs, to acquire an asset for improved income generation, or to begin saving and thereby achieving some level of resilience. The graduation models provide short-term relief and a window of opportunity to do better. In some cases, it may take people from the most abject situation to something slightly better (such as when improved savings practices allows people to become more resilient in the face of crises, or so it would seem). Can the poorest people graduate to something even better?

On the other hand, in market development models, we seek integration into market systems that empower the poor, and, in some few cases, the poorest, to become viable economic actors. Sometimes this appears to work very well, and other times not.

In our own arrogance, I do not think that we understand when these approaches will and will not work – we just want to help, and perhaps therein lies the problem (paternalism).

This comes back to the fact that these are not really 'economic models' at all, but ideas that are generally not proven by hard evidence. Not that we can believe in economic models either – we have heard the debates around structural adjustments, the 'broken window fallacy' and trickle-down theory – indeed, economists rarely agree with one another.

So, Ben, with some trepidation, I am making the assertion that our current models cannot help the poorest (and perhaps even the poor). I look forward to your counter argument.

Ben Fowler: Before I address your assertions, let me point out a few areas of agreement. I do agree that we have struggled to even reach – let alone benefit – the poorest with many of our traditional models. I do, however, feel more strongly that we are doing better at making progress in this difficult yet critical endeavour than you do.

I believe you are making three assertions. First, that negative global trends suggest we are making little difference on the lives of the poorest. Second, that graduation models make only differences at the margins. And third, that we have little real evidence for our approaches and thus cannot really speak of models at all. I will address each of these in turn.

With respect to your first argument, I believe the global trends actually point to an overall reduction in the quantity of the very poor. Though income is a very imperfect measure, World Bank statistics show the number of people living on less than US$1.25 per day has dropped on an absolute basis, from 1.9 billion in 1981 to 1.29 billion in 2008. The decline as a percentage of the world's population is even clearer. While our ability to claim attribution for these changes is stronger in some cases than others, I would suggest the trend is more positive than you indicate. Speaking at a global level can sometimes obscure more than it illustrates, so therefore let's examine the experiences of the graduation models that you mention.

Graduation models reflect significant learning by NGOs, academia, donors, and governments about what has and has not worked in supporting the very poor. These models reflect the fact that food, cash, or asset transfers alone are helpful but rarely sustainable, while the very poor are rarely able to participate in value-chain development, microfinance, and other strategies that require substantial risk tolerance and assets. Sequencing strategies steadily build the capacity of very poor households to take risks and invest in new opportunities by building assets, diversifying income sources, and improving financial literacy. This is a sensible approach. While many graduation schemes are still pilots, BRAC's work on targeting the ultra-poor with a series of interventions since 2002 reduced the number of households living on less than half a dollar per day from 85 per cent to 8 per cent.

Perhaps you do not consider these graduation models to be models as such, given that their specific components vary between contexts. I think, however, that this is actually a strength, reflecting the very differing realities faced by the poor, and the importance of the social context. Further, some components are common across most graduation programming, suggesting they are critical to supporting graduation. Asset building is one such element. Facilitating savings groups or their equivalent, for example, can have substantial impacts upon the ability of the very poor to plan their expenditures. Savings group members in one pilot I visited described with considerable passion the impacts they had observed in their ability to save and invest. As such platforms build the resiliency of the very poor to shocks, other programming, including linkages to markets, becomes relevant.

Such examples suggest that the poorest can indeed be helped by our economic development models. The scale of the problem, however, suggests an urgency to our efforts to make those models more scalable and cost-effective.

Linda Jones: Thank you for your response and your analysis of my comments on global trends, graduation models, and evidence. This is a useful way to continue the conversation.

With regard to global trends and statistics, my concern here is that it all depends on what and whose statistics you use. For example, the FAO estimated in 2010 that 925 million people (13.6 per cent of the world's population) were undernourished and that this number had increased since 1995–97 (including before the food crisis when the figure peaked). According to the FAO, this increase is due to three factors: the neglect of the agricultural sector, the worldwide economic situation, and the increases in food prices from a range of causes.

These seemingly contradictory sets of statistics indicate that our analysis is flawed – and can be used in our arguments to support whatever side we are taking. Our definitions are equally flawed, and perhaps blinkered. As an aside, let's look at human trafficking. Do the human slaves that are trafficked all over the world ever make it to the statistics of the poorest? Certainly, our approaches are not reaching these people as far as I know – so what do we even mean when we say 'the poorest'? The ILO estimates that there are over 12 million slaves in the world at any one time (other estimates are higher); in India, there are estimated to be 3 million prostitutes of which 40 per cent are children and, by definition, trafficked; in our 'first world Canada' approximately 2,000 people are trafficked through our borders to the US annually, and 600–800 are living as slaves within our borders. On one level, you may argue that these numbers are not germane to this discussion – but to me they are about the bigger question of who are the poorest and are we reaching them with our programmes and our measurements?

Graduation models represent an interesting approach, and certainly a valuable response to the 'no subsidy' thinking that dominated the debate for some time. There are hopeful experiences and pilots. It will be interesting to see what they accomplish in the long run as programmes such as BRAC's that you reference are scaled up and measured over time. However, I remember visiting fair trade groups in India – people who had gone from ultra-poor to poor (up to about \$2 per day). These groups worked long hours but were thrilled because they had decent working conditions, could feed their families, and could even take their kids out of government schools. It was a graduation from deep poverty to manageable poverty (at that place and at that time). Perhaps I am not easily pleased, however, because I just have to wonder – is this the best we can do?

Which brings us to the last point – a real sticking point for the whole industry: evidence. What do we really know? If the FAO is right that there are more malnourished people in the world than ever – despite World Bank evidence of income increases – then what is the 'reality' of people's situation? Look at the debates in the microfinance industry over who has really benefited and to what extent? How far do any of our projects measure beyond the life of the interventions? Are the changes that we have seen sustainable? What happens when there is a change in government, a change in consumer trends, a new tax, a natural disaster? We are so eager to talk about success stories that we gloss over issues and pat ourselves on the back. New measurement approaches are taking hold (MEDA's livelihoods measures, the DCED Standard, Most Significant Change) and perhaps we will demonstrate change more convincingly over time.

Ben, this is not to disparage people's efforts and the success stories that do exist, but to support meaningful debate. We are trying new things as an industry: graduation models, projects that combine food security and income outcomes, women's agricultural leadership and empowerment. This is all good, and I applaud the work even while I ask these questions.

Ben Fowler: You raise some very helpful challenges and clarifications. Certainly, the evidence can be contradictory and I would be the first to agree that income-based measures do not provide the full story of socio-economic status;

I doubt there is any single metric that can. Nevertheless, we have moved a long way as a field from conceiving of the poor as a single group of people and assuming they are benefiting from our programming without ever testing that assumption. Many microfinance institutions and value-chain initiatives are recognizing the importance of understanding the poverty levels of their clients and are integrating this into their market assessments, monitoring, and evaluation systems. Efforts are being made to design practical tools that support this.

Some of these combine standard measures (e.g. comparison against a national poverty line) with subjective ones (e.g. community identification of the poorest households). Moreover, the SEEP Network has just launched a new initiative, STEP-UP, that will be addressing the issue of terminology, in the recognition that it can be fraught with challenges.

Your example of the Indian fair trade group members suggests we agree our models can indeed help the poorest, but that we need to look at what more can be done. I certainly think there is a lot more we can do. While I can't speak to your specific example, I think we need to see these changes as being one step on a path that leads to economic well-being, and that, particularly for the most vulnerable and poorest, this can take time, with setbacks along the way. The $2 per day they are now earning should not be seen as the end goal, but is nevertheless a very substantial improvement from the starting point. I see that as the very essence of what graduation models are trying to accomplish: steadily improving households' well-being while recognizing this is not an immediate jump.

Certainly there are risks of these advances being reversed, and the poorest are frequently the most vulnerable to such shocks. Some of these risks – drought, illness, or death of a family income earner – are ones that can be mitigated in part or in full by household-level risk management strategies. Building resilience to address common shocks such as these should be an important consideration in our programming. Addressing some of these challenges does certainly go beyond what our models alone can deliver, and points to the need for an approach that includes broader safety nets.

There is certainly a need to build a more robust evidence base on what works and what does not, particularly in how to effectively reach scale. This issue is, of course, not exclusive to our debate topic but relates to nearly any area of development, unfortunately. Many graduation models have naturally approached their efforts as a pilot in order to inform future scale-up. As they begin to do so, we will need to assess their effectiveness carefully.

I believe we both agree the poorest *can* be helped by our current models of economic development, but that we have a lot more work still to do to ensure these efforts are scalable and sustainable.

Update

Linda Jones: It is very interesting to me to renew the debate that we started three years ago. I feel torn – on the one hand more hopeful, but on the other hand less so.

For the world in general, and therefore for the poor in particular, I come to this debate with a heavy heart. I think of many of the places where our readers, you and I have worked or continue to work – Ukraine, Gaza, Syria, South Sudan, Pakistan, Philippines, Haiti – and the list goes on. Countries that have been beset by conflict, corruption, climate change and natural disasters, where local and international development efforts have been devastated, and the lives of citizens have been thrown into turmoil – or worse. I also think of the rising intolerance in some of the developed countries towards new citizens who are often a small percentage of the population with fewer resources, but are labelled and persecuted. While at the same time, the official count for refugees, those who would find a home, has reached 50 million – the highest since the Second World War.

And yet, despite this terrible record, I think our field – 'microfinance and enterprise development' or 'inclusive financial services' and 'market systems development' as many of us name our work now – have developed tools and capacities that can contribute more than ever to sustainable, scalable and inclusive development.

The savings group revolution and the implementation of graduation models that you identified in 2012 have both come a long way with evidence of success – for example, there are more than 10 million people now engaged in savings groups, and there has been the formalization of new models such as 'push–pull' described elsewhere in this volume. Moreover, innovation is catching fire; innovation is no longer just a buzzword when applied to development practice, but is being pursued rigorously and with resources from donors and foundations. And, not just innovation in technology and mobile telephony, although those are certainly important aspects of innovation: innovation in finance is gaining ground through public–private partnerships, viable impact investing, development impact bonds, and more and stronger social enterprises. Further, innovation in programme design is also on the rise, driven in part by finance and new technologies, but also by experience and creativity, the willingness to partner with the private sector, and a wider recognition that the role of sustainable development is to support rather than direct local institutions.

There are of course still vulnerable populations that we are not doing a great job of integrating into financial and market systems. For example, we are paying much more attention to women's roles in economic development but there is a long way to go. Women often remain invisible in agriculture particularly when a crop is perceived to be in a man's domain. But what is often overlooked is the painstaking work of women on those very crops in activities such as post-harvest handling. The quality of outputs could be greatly improved and workloads drastically reduced if some simple (and often known) technologies were introduced. But if a role is invisible, a solution will not be forthcoming, and women continue to spend tireless hours sorting, peeling, drying, etc. but do not receive support or recognition from development programmes while the focus remains largely on financing and distributing inputs and creating market linkages.

Other marginalized groups – people with disabilities, ethnic minorities, rural youth, the destitute – are usually excluded because they are not seen either, their current or potential contributions are not recognized, the efforts required for integration are perceived as too great, or a society actively spurns these people.

Ultimately, to achieve our goals of inclusive, scalable and sustainable development, disabling environments will need to be rectified. Countries that wish to include the poor and vulnerable will have to overcome constraints relating to transparency, corruption, civil unrest, extremism, legal frameworks, regulation and enforcement, and socio-cultural barriers. The wealth of a nation is not enough to guarantee this and middle-income status does not necessarily eliminate or even reduce poverty.

Work at the grassroots and the policy levels are both important; it is not an either/or but a continuum. As Kavita Ramdas recounted in her 2009 TedTalk what a Filipina activist once said to her, 'How do you cook a rice cake? With heat from the bottom and heat from the top.'

Ben Fowler: Revisiting our discussions with the benefit of time offers the opportunity to reflect on what we thought then in the light of new research and experiences. It is exciting to contemplate many of the forces that you cite. Indeed, the recognition that very simple, locally managed savings groups can be such a powerful tool for smoothing consumption among vulnerable populations has been quite a positive step. And several other models such as impact investing seem promising though their impact to benefit the vulnerable at scale still remains to be proven in many contexts.

I would like to highlight two areas where practitioners such as ourselves who are focused on market systems and financial systems development have paid arguably too little attention, and yet are worthy of our focus. The first is cash transfers. I am surprised that we made no mention of these mechanisms during our last discussion, in spite of the interest that they had already attracted. At this stage, it would be quite a mistake to repeat the omission. As you know, cash transfers (CTs) are often made on a regular basis to vulnerable households in countries such as India. Also, there is growing evidence to suggest that CTs can provide both non-economic (e.g. educational, health and nutritional) benefits to recipient households. For instance, studies have found that receiving CTs is correlated with a reduction in risky sexual behaviour among females, educational attendance and health outcomes. What is particularly exciting about CTs to me is their potential for scale in reaching the most vulnerable; they are widely recognized as an extremely cost-effective mechanism, particularly if institutionalized. So how can we use these platforms? It seems to me that our field can add value in understanding how these regular cash infusions can contribute to long-term economic transformation among participant households. Some initiatives are now combining payments with other services, such as vocational training and small business support as described in the introduction to this volume (Jones, 2015).

A second area that I want to flag is the role of labour. For a long time, our focus has been on targeting and measuring the impacts of our work on entrepreneurs, and particularly microentrepreneurs. We have anticipated (though not always confirmed) that in many cases the poor are the very microenterprise owners that we target. Yet while this approach of creating economic opportunities for these enterprises is extremely important, we often lose sight of the fact that many of the world's extreme poor do not own productive assets like farmland. Rather, they toil as labourers for others, traditionally in agriculture but increasingly in other sectors. In fact rural wage labour is the most important form of employment for the very poorest households. In my opinion, this is only going to grow with time and is a priority for our sector. In some cases, our assumptions that those vulnerable workers will benefit from improvements in the enterprises are not born out by research. For example, the disbursement of fair trade earnings from farmer to worker are unclear and may not be as beneficial as thought. This thus poses a challenge, but also an exciting new opportunity for us to better understand the tools and approaches that can effectively reach wage workers. Of course, this is easier said than done. It is relatively easy to design interventions that those with assets can seize, and relatively difficult to reach those who lack assets. Nevertheless, economic trends suggest this will be increasingly where poor and vulnerable populations are active, and thus where we will increasingly need to focus.

About the authors

Linda Jones is an internationally recognized consultant in applying market systems approaches (value chains, financial systems, M4P, PSD) to inclusive economic development programmes that successfully leverage the contributions of women, smallholder farmers and other vulnerable groups. Dr Jones works globally with multiple clients and donors, and is currently directing MEDA's work in investment-led development.

References

Narayan, Deepa, Patel, Raj, Schafft, Kai, Rademacher, Anne, and Koch-Schulte, Sarah (2000) *Voices of the Poor: Can Anyone Hear Us?* Oxford: Oxford University Press and Washington, World Bank.

Ramdas, Kavita (2009) 'Radical Women Embracing Tradition' Mysore, India, Ted Talk, <https://www.ted.com/talks/kavita_ramdas_radical_women_embracing_tradition> [last accessed 23 March 2015].

CHAPTER 12

Conclusions: the way ahead for including the poorest

Linda Jones

Abstract

Support for programmes involving the poorest and most vulnerable may be affected by diminishing funding: international development funding in the post-2015 era is projected to falter. Climate change and other enabling environment factors may also impact on the poorest. Nevertheless, there is general consensus that poverty is overall declining over the last 30 years. There are also innovations that offer promise for microfinance and enterprise development programmes that attempt to reach very poor and vulnerable people.

Keywords: post-2015 funding; climate change; income poverty

Integrating the vulnerable into financial and market systems requires new models, additional resources and focused efforts of development agencies, governments and donors. Progress has been made, and new approaches have shown success for inclusive development.

Funding projections

Unfortunately, there are some red flags on the horizon (MEDA, 2014). According to the Organisation for Economic Co-operation and Development (OECD) pre-release report on spending in the post-2015 period, there will be reduced allocations for poverty reduction and greater focus on economic growth by donors (OECD, 2014). The 2014 edition of the survey collected information from all DAC members (29 members who are high-income country donors, with the latest being UAE), the largest 25 multilateral agencies and 6 additional countries. The pre-release report finds, for example, that aid to Africa is projected to decline and two-thirds of the countries in sub-Saharan Africa will receive less in 2017 than today, with worrying consequences for growing populations living in countries that have failed to meet the Millennium Development Goals. The largest increases are projected for middle-income Asian countries, such as India, Jordan and Pakistan (as well as a few low-income countries: Bangladesh, Cambodia and Nepal) with overall allocations to Asia expected to equal those towards Africa by 2017. In Europe and the Americas, donations were expected

http://dx.doi.org/10.3362/9781780448879.012

to be less by the end of 2014 and stagnant in the following years, and overall contributions are expected to hover around US$100 billion per year for country programme aid, which is the level realized in 2013 after rebounding from the post-financial crisis recession (OECD, 2014).

Moreover, local, national and international enabling environments may be the greatest hurdle of all. We have seen incredible upheavals in recent years that have undone many decades of development: the financial crisis, conflicts and extremism, corruption, climate change and natural disasters. Although these challenges cannot be overcome by development programming alone, we can and are doing more to influence change and support resiliency in the face of these challenges.

Overall income poverty in the world has declined – the World Bank (2013) reports that in the past 30 years, the number of people living under $1.25 (PPP) per day in the developing world decreased from over half to less than a quarter of the total population, which rose by 59 per cent during the same period. And, although these may be optimistic statistics,[1] there is general consensus that poverty is overall down (with the caveat that unchecked environmental degradation and climate change may shift this trend in coming years). At the same time, our brave new world of massive technological, social and financial innovation holds the potential for dramatic solutions, which, with the will of public and private sector actors, can be turned into realities on the ground.

We also know that by both the HDI and MPI measures, poverty is on the decrease, and some countries have made great strides: for example, several countries across Africa, Asia and Latin America are success stories for MPI poverty reduction – e.g. Nepal and Rwanda lead in achievement, followed by Ghana, Tanzania, Uganda, Bangladesh, Cambodia and Bolivia – with the greatest reductions in low income or LDC countries. In fact, India is the only MPI-reporting country where the disparity between rich and poor has continued to grow (Alkire and Vaz, 2014), although with a shifting funder landscape and increased corporate and private philanthropy, India may be positioned to clean up its act.[2]

Innovation

New and rapid advances in technology, alternative forms of finance, and new partnerships offer opportunities to reduce poverty and include the vulnerable in financial and market systems.

For example, we see donors pushing the envelope on innovation – from USAID's Global Development Lab (USAID, 2015) to DFID's Amplify programme (2015). Development programmes are restructuring to promote innovation such as the Accion Venture Lab (2015), while others are focused on technology solutions for the poorest such as the Bill and Melinda Gates Foundation's work in mobile money for the poor (2015).

New forms of finance are also being used to reach objectives: blended finance, impact investing, crowdfunding, social impact bonds and more. Innovations in finance are bringing more private sector money into play, often utilizing donor funding as catalytic or concessionary finance to attract private investment for long-term sustainable development. Such finance, for example, is being used to promote SME growth that leads to job creation and supply chain development (e.g. involving smallholder farmers) that impacts the poor.

In this context, microfinance and enterprise development programmes continue to be significant contributors to poverty reduction for the most vulnerable. Initiatives such as those described in this book give us hope – that we are skilled enough and confident enough to move to the next level of programming, to adopt and to create innovations, and to target the hardest to reach with sustainable initiatives that allow even the most vulnerable to become the drivers of their own development.

About the author

Linda Jones is an internationally recognized consultant in applying market systems approaches (value chains, financial systems, M4P, PSD) to inclusive economic development programmes that successfully leverage the contributions of women, smallholder farmers and other vulnerable groups. Dr Jones works globally with multiple clients and donors, and is currently directing MEDA's work in investment-led development.

Endnotes

1. Although, not to be overly cynical, there are questions about the statistics. See for example: http://www.globalissues.org/article/26/poverty-facts-and-stats and http://mdgs.un.org/unsd/mdg/Metadata.aspx?IndicatorId=0&SeriesId=580
2. See for example: http://samhita.org/philanthropy-landscape-in-india-csr-and-beyond/; http://www.bain.com/publications/articles/india-philanthropy-report-2013.aspx; and http://www.mensxp.com/special-features/today/3876-warren-buffett-and-bill-gates-in-india-to-give-tutorials-in-charity.html

References

ACCION (2014) 'Venture Lab' <https://www.accion.org/venturelab> [Accessed 4 March 2015].

Alkire, S. and Vaz. A. (2014) 'Reducing Multidimensional Poverty and Destitution'. Technical note, Oxford, OPHI <http://www.ophi.org.uk/wp-content/uploads/ReducingMultidimensionalPovertyandDestitution-PaceandPatterns.pdf?0a8fd7> [Accessed 3 February 2015].

Bill and Melinda Gates Foundation (2015) 'Mobile banking will help the poor transform their lives' in *Our big bet for the future* <http://www.gatesnotes.com/2015-annual-letter?page=3&lang=en&WT.mc_id=01_21_2015_AL2015-GF_GFO_domain_Top_21> [Accessed 4 March 2015].

DFID (2015) 'Amplify open innovation for development' <http://devtracker. dfid.gov.uk/projects/GB-1-203798/> [Accessed 4 March 2015].

OECD (2014) 'Pre-Release of Findings from the Upcoming 2014 OECD Report on the Global Outlook on Aid' <http://www.oecd.org/dac/aid-architecture/ Global%20Outlook%20on%20Aid%20Predictability_WEB.pdf> [Accessed 4 February 2015].

USAID (2015) 'About the U.S. Global development lab' <http://www.usaid. gov/GlobalDevLab/about> [Accessed 4 March 2015].

World Bank (2013) 'Remarkable declines in global poverty, but major challenges remain', Washington D.C., World Bank <http://www.worldbank.org/en/ news/press-release/2013/04/17/remarkable-declines-in-global-poverty-but- major-challenges-remain> [Accessed 3 February 2015].

www.ingramcontent.com/pod-product-compliance
Lightning Source LLC
Chambersburg PA
CBHW072105040426
42334CB00042B/2463